ÉCLAIRS

ÉCLAIRS

Easy, Elegant & Modern Recipes

Christophe Adam

Robert
ROSE

Éclairs

Originally published under the title *Les Éclairs* © 2015, Éditions de La Martinière, une marque de la société EDLM (Paris)

Translation copyright © 2017 Robert Rose Inc.

Cover and text design copyright © 2017 Robert Rose Inc.

Photographs copyright © 2015 Éditions de La Martinière, une marque de la société EDLM (Paris)

For complete cataloguing information, see page 223.

Disclaimer

The recipes in this book have been carefully tested by our kitchen and our tasters. To the best of our knowledge, they are safe and nutritious for ordinary use and users. For those people with food or other allergies, or who have special food requirements or health issues, please read the suggested contents of each recipe carefully and determine whether or not they may create a problem for you. All recipes are used at the risk of the consumer.

We cannot be responsible for any hazards, loss or damage that may occur as a result of any recipe use.

For those with special needs, allergies, requirements or health problems, in the event of any doubt, please contact your medical adviser prior to the use of any recipe.

Translator: Donna Vekteris

Editor: Meredith Dees

Recipe Editor: Jennifer MacKenzie

Proofreader: Gillian Watts

Indexer: Gillian Watts

Design and production: Alicia McCarthy & Kevin Cockburn/PageWave Graphics Inc.

Photography: Rina Nurra

Page layout adapted from *Les Éclairs*, designed by Justeciel Conception Graphique

The publisher gratefully acknowledges the financial support of our publishing program by the Government of Canada through the Canada Book Fund.

Canadä

Published by Robert Rose Inc.

120 Eglinton Avenue East, Suite 800, Toronto, Ontario, Canada M4P 1E2

Tel: (416) 322-6552 Fax: (416) 322-6936

www.robertrose.ca

Printed and bound in China

4 5 6 7 8 9 ESP 25 24 23 22

AUTHOR'S NOTE

You may think that this is yet another book on éclairs.
But treat this one as more of a private lesson in
your own kitchen with me by your side.

The éclair is an exercise in style that I have been
perfecting for over twelve years. To me, the éclair is
a gourmet delight that allows me to marry fruits, flavors
and textures in unlimited creative fashion.

With more than twenty inventive recipes on top of some
fifteen basic ones, I promise you will have plenty to please
everyone, from family and friends to formal guests.

This book will help you practice all the basics until
you are comfortable inventing your own recipes.

A final word of advice: be pragmatic and creative,
and all your éclairs, from classic to ultra-chic,
are destined for greatness.

— *Christophe Adam*

CONTENTS

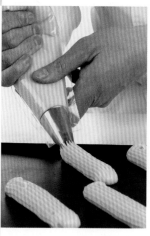

» Chocolate
Crunch
Éclairs
89

» Hazelnut
Praline
Éclairs
97

« Caramel
Peanut Éclairs
103

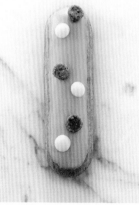

« Lemon
Éclairs
113

» Raspberry-
Cherry
Sugared
Almond
Éclairs
123

» Valentine
Heart Éclairs
131

« Fig Éclairs
139

« Strawberry
Éclairs
147

GETTING STARTED

Ingredients

- **Chocolate:** Buy the best quality chocolate and compound chocolate possible for the truest flavor and best texture. The pistoles or callets make for easy weighing and use since they don't need further chopping before melting.

- **Clear glaze:** A thickened glucose syrup product designed for glazing pastries, called a mirror glaze or piping gel. It is available at cake decorating supply stores, craft and bulk stores with a baking section and online. Be sure the product you buy can be warmed.

- **Food color:** Powdered food color is specified in some recipes, but in general any paste or gel will work as well. For the most vivid results, look for high-quality, intense colors at cake decorating supply stores and at craft and bulk stores with a baking section and online. Remember a little goes a long way when adding to choux pastry and glazes.

- **Fruit purées:** Look for prepared fruit purées at confectionery or cake decorating supply stores and online. Choose a product with natural fruit and as few added ingredients as possible. If using a frozen product, let it thaw completely before adding to your recipe.

- **Shimmer powder or luster dust:** These are very fine powders in vivid colors and metallics. They are available at confectionery and cake decorating supply stores, some well-stocked craft stores and online

Equipment

- Kitchen scale
- Saucepan
- Mixing bowl
- Large fine-mesh sieves
- Fine-mesh sieves
- Wooden spoon
- Whisk
- Heatproof silicone spatula
- Offset palette knife
- Straight palette knife
- Bowl scraper
- Immersion blender
- Large round pastry brush
- Flat pastry brush
- Pastry bag and piping tips (round and star/fluted)
- Sharp knives
- Toothbrush (clean)
- Fine-tooth grater or citrus zester (such as a Microplane rasp)
- Rolling pin
- Tuile mold
- Silicone baking mat
- Candy thermometer
- Instant-read thermometer

Tips For Making Lavish Gourmet Éclairs

Making éclairs is an exercise in style that requires a certain amount of skill. There are, however, a few simple rules that will help you succeed every time!

Basics

- Before you begin a recipe, carefully read the recipe step by step and prepare all of the ingredients you will need.

- Read the recipe several times if necessary to be sure you have understood all of the steps. Remember that most creams and glazes must be made the day before!

- Always use an immersion blender to mix your glaze after reheating it. This helps to remove air bubbles and results in a smooth and shiny finish.

Ingredients

- Always use high-quality ingredients.

- You can find the main ingredients and fresh produce you will need at your favorite grocery stores. The rest of the ingredients can be found at baking and cake-decorating supply stores and through specialized websites—see page 17.

- Always use whole milk products, not fat-free or low-fat versions. If you don't, your cream won't set.

- When you need to add food coloring, it's better to use the gel, paste or powdered form. The color will be purer and you will avoid adding liquid to the glaze, which could alter its texture. However, if you only have liquid food coloring on hand and add only a few drops, the result will be just as satisfactory.

- When measuring ingredients for these recipes, be sure to use one set of measurements, either U.S. volumes and weights or metric volumes and weights; do not use a combination, as that can change proportions, leading to failed recipes. The metric weights are included for main ingredients, so if you have kitchen scales, it's recommended to use weights for optimal accuracy.

Equipment

- Making éclairs does not require using a lot of equipment, but certain items are essential—see page 19.

- To ensure perfect results, pipe your éclairs using a star (fluted) tip that is best suited to the size of éclairs you are making (see page 33).

- To facilitate handling and avoid having a lot of dishes to wash, use disposable plastic pastry bags to pipe your cream. These bags also allow you to cut the exact size of hole to fit the tip you need for piping (small for filling éclairs through the holes in their base, larger for other types of filling).

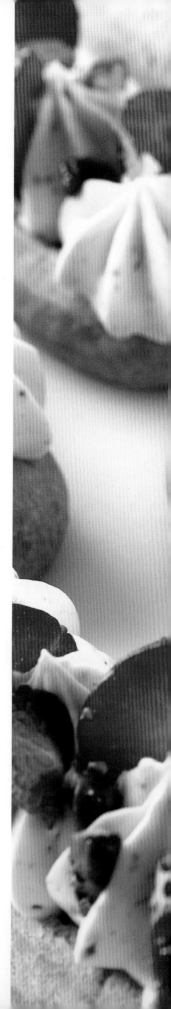

Storage

- Choux pastry keeps very well in the freezer. You can make a large quantity and freeze it in portions.

- Glaze will keep for up to two weeks in the refrigerator (cover the surface of the glaze with plastic wrap).

- All chocolate decorations can be made several days in advance and stored in an airtight container in a cool, dry place.

- The filled and decorated éclairs themselves are best eaten the same day you make them, but you can also serve them the day after, if needed. Store in an airtight container and refrigerate overnight.

For Every Taste...

- Don't be afraid to use your imagination and vary the colors and decorations on your éclairs.

- You can add flavor to your glazes by adding a few drops of pure extract, such as vanilla, almond, lemon or orange.

- Since glaze keeps well, consider preparing clear glaze in advance that you can color or flavor according to your needs as you make your éclairs.

BASIC RECIPES

Choux Pastry

MAKES 1½ LBS (750 G) PASTRY

Enough for 20 classic éclairs, 50 small éclairs or 120 miniature éclairs

Preparation time: 30 minutes

EQUIPMENT

- Large baking sheet(s), lined with parchment paper or silicone baking mat

- Preheat oven to 350°F (175°C)

CHOUX PASTRY

⅔ cup	water	150 mL
⅔ cup	whole milk	150 mL
1¾ tsp	pure vanilla extract	8 mL
1½ tsp	granulated sugar	7 mL
¾ cup	unsalted butter, cut into small pieces (160 g)	175 mL
¾ tsp	salt	3 mL
1 cup + 3 tbsp	all-purpose flour (160 g)	295 mL
5	large eggs, beaten (approx.)	5

COLORED PASTRY

1	batch choux pastry	1
	Food coloring (your choice of color)	

1 CHOUX PASTRY

In a medium saucepan, combine water, milk, vanilla, sugar, butter and salt.

Bring to a boil over medium heat.

Remove from heat. Add flour.

Using a wooden spoon, stir until flour is completely incorporated and dough pulls away from sides of pan, leaving sides of pan fairly clean.

6

Return pan to medium-low heat. Cook dough, stirring continuously with a wooden spoon or heatproof spatula, for 5 minutes, until dough is smooth and forms a ball. (Heating the dough like this helps to "dry it out" so you end up with a uniform mixture that is not too moist.)

7

Transfer mixture to a bowl. Gradually add just enough egg to make a glossy, firm dough, while beating well with a wooden spoon or heatproof spatula—this is essential for the pastry to turn out well.

8

The dough will be very smooth and hold its shape.

9

COLORED CHOUX PASTRY

Prepare pastry dough following Steps 1 to 9.

Add a small amount of food coloring to pastry dough, then, using a silicone spatula, stir until evenly incorporated. Gradually add more coloring until desired shade is reached.

3 PIPING AND BAKING ÉCLAIRS

Using bowl scraper or spatula, transfer dough to a pastry bag fitted with a ¾-inch (2 cm) star tip. On prepared baking sheet(s), pipe pastry dough into oblong shapes, spacing about 2 inches (5 cm) apart (they will expand as they bake): *Classic éclairs:* 5¼ by 1 inch (13 by 2.5 cm); *Small éclairs:* 2½ by ¾ inch (6 by 1.5 cm); *Miniature éclairs:* 2 by ½ inch (5 by 1 cm).

Bake one sheet at a time, in preheated oven until evenly puffed and golden brown and they feel hollow: *Classic éclairs:* 35 minutes; *Small éclairs:* 30 minutes; *Miniature éclairs:* 25 minutes. Do not open oven door while baking, or éclairs will collapse. At the end of baking, turn oven off, open oven door about ½ inch (1 cm) and let cool for 15 minutes (they will continue to brown slightly) to let steam escape and prevent éclairs from cracking. Transfer to racks to cool completely.

Craquelin Éclairs

<table>
<tr><td>MAKES
10 CLASSIC ÉCLAIRS</td></tr>
</table>

Preparation time: 30 minutes

EQUIPMENT

- Rolling pin
- Straight palette knife
- Ruler
- Large baking sheet, lined with parchment paper or silicone baking mat

CRAQUELIN

⅓ cup	unsalted butter, cut into cubes, softened	75 mL
7 tbsp	packed brown sugar (100 g)	105 mL
¾ cup	all-purpose flour, sifted (100 g)	175 mL

CHOUX PASTRY

1	batch Choux Pastry (page 29)	1

1

3

In a bowl, using a wooden spoon, mash together butter and brown sugar.

Add flour and stir just until a smooth dough forms (be careful not to overwork). Cover and refrigerate for at least 2 hours.

4

5

6

Place chilled dough between 2 sheets of parchment paper (to prevent dough from sticking) on work surface. Roll out dough into a large square about $\frac{1}{16}$ inch (2 mm) thick. Slide dough, still between parchment, onto a rimless baking sheet and refrigerate for 1 hour, until firm.

Remove top sheet of parchment paper. Using a sharp knife, cut dough into 1-inch (2.5 cm) strips. Cut strips into squares. Transfer to an airtight container and refrigerate until ready to use. Any leftover craquelin dough will keep for up to 3 days.

CHOUX PASTRY

Prepare choux pastry following Steps 1 to 9 on pages 30 and 31.

ASSEMBLY AND BAKING

Preheat oven to 350°F (175°C).

Using bowl scraper or spatula, fill pastry bag fitted with a ½-inch (1 cm) round piping tip.

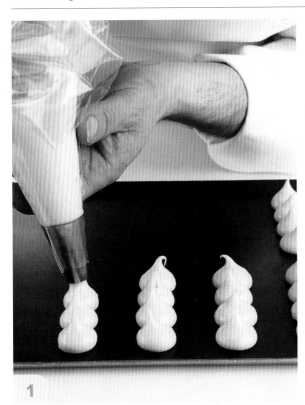

1

2

On prepared baking sheet, for each éclair, pipe four 1-inch (2.5 cm) mounds of pastry in a straight line so they are touching each other slightly. Repeat, spacing éclairs at least 2 inches (5 cm) apart (they will expand as they bake), to make 10 éclairs.

Using palette knife or a paring knife, gently place 1 square of craquelin dough on top of each mound of pastry. Bake in preheated oven for 30 minutes, until evenly puffed and golden brown and éclairs feel hollow (they will continue to brown slightly). Do not open oven door while baking or éclairs will collapse. At the end of baking, turn oven off, open oven door about ½ inch (1 cm) and let cool for 15 minutes to let steam escape and prevent éclairs from cracking. Transfer to racks to cool completely.

Chocolate Shells

**MAKES 10
CHOCOLATE SHELLS**

| 1 lb 5 oz | dark (60%) chocolate, couverture pistoles or chopped, divided | 600 g |

Preparation time: 1 hour

EQUIPMENT

- Immersion blender
- Wide, flat pastry brush
- Offset palette knife
- Tuile mold

TEMPLATE

- Cardstock rectangle, about 1 inch (2.5 cm) larger than size of éclair
- Chocolate transfer sheets (your choice)

---

1 TEMPLATE

1

Trace an oblong shape the same size as your éclairs onto cardstock, and then cut out. Use the template to cut out 10 oblongs from the chocolate transfer sheet.

2 CHOCOLATE SHELLS

In a heatproof bowl set over a pan of simmering water or in top of a double boiler over low heat, melt 14 oz (400 g) chocolate. Stir until smooth, then remove from heat.

1

2

Add remaining 7 oz (200 g) chocolate and stir until completely melted.

Using immersion blender, blend melted chocolate until smooth. (If bowl is too shallow, transfer chocolate to a warmed tall cup to blend.)

3

4

5

Lay chocolate transfer cutouts printed-side-up on a clean work surface (preferably very smooth marble or other smooth surface). Dip pastry brush in chocolate to coat thickly, then drizzle melted chocolate from brush onto each cutout. Using offset palette knife, spread chocolate evenly all over transfer sheet in a very thin layer, letting chocolate extend slightly over the edges. Set aside to let shapes cool slightly (but not until completely solid).

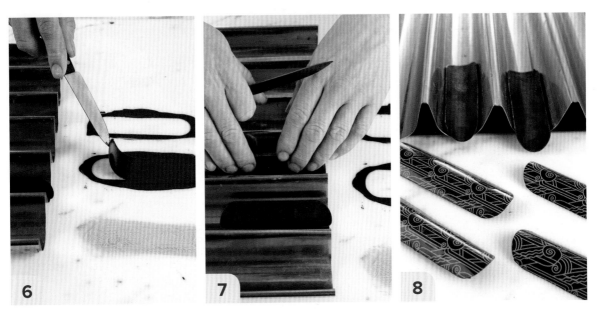

6

7

8

Using the tip of a paring knife, gently lift each chocolate shell, with the transfer sheet, from work surface, leaving rough edges behind, and place print-side-down in tuile mold to make a curved shape.

Refrigerate for at least 10 minutes, until chocolate has hardened.

9

10

Peel plastic film from transfer sheet covering chocolate shells, then place shell, decorated side up, on filled and glazed (if using) éclairs.

Chocolate Drizzle Decorations

MAKES 10 DECORATIONS		

Preparation time: 45 minutes

10 oz	milk chocolate, pistoles or chopped, divided	300 g

EQUIPMENT

- Cardstock rectangle, about 1 inch (2.5 cm) larger than size of éclair
- 1 sheet thick plastic to cut template
- Permanent marker
- Utility knife
- Instant-read thermometer
- Immersion blender
- Disposable pastry bag (uncut)

◼ 1 TEMPLATE

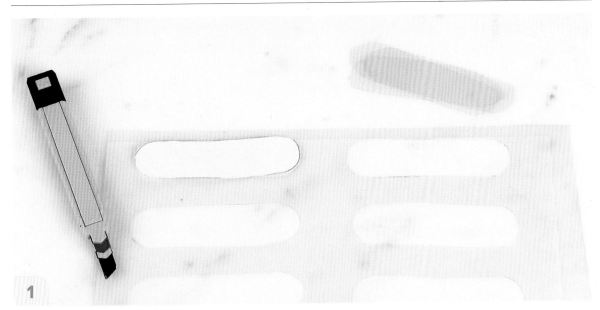

Trace an oblong shape the same size as your éclairs onto cardstock, then cut out. Using marker, trace 10 oblongs (or as many as you can fit) onto plastic sheet, leaving at least 1 inch (2.5 cm) between each. Using utility knife, cut out the oblongs, leaving the sheet intact (you will be using the holes).

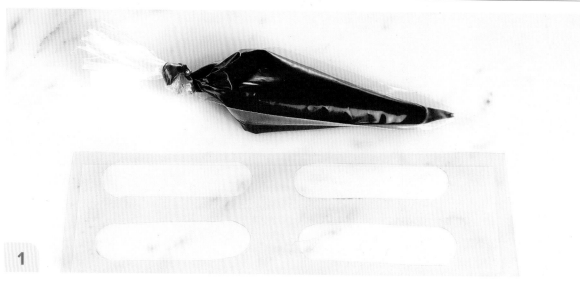

1

In a heatproof bowl set over a pan of simmering water or in top of a double boiler over low heat, melt 7 oz (200 g) chocolate, stirring occasionally. When temperature of the chocolate registers 104°F (40°C) on instant-read thermometer, remove from heat and add remaining 3 oz (100 g) chocolate. Stir until chocolate is completely melted. Using immersion blender, blend until smooth. (If bowl is too shallow, transfer chocolate to a warmed tall cup to blend.) Using spatula, transfer chocolate to pastry bag. Snip off tip of pastry bag so that only a thin stream of chocolate can be squeezed out.

2

3

Lay a sheet of plastic wrap, parchment paper or silicone baking mat on a clean work surface. Place plastic template on top. Using filled pastry bag, draw chocolate zigzags over length and width of holes in the template, extending over edges of holes slightly.

Working quickly (you don't want chocolate to harden), gently peel up template and discard (or save to use again).

4

5

Carefully slide plastic wrap with chocolate shapes on it to a rimless baking sheet. Refrigerate for 30 minutes, until chocolate has hardened.

6

7

Gently place one chocolate decoration on top of each of your glazed éclairs.

Filling Éclairs

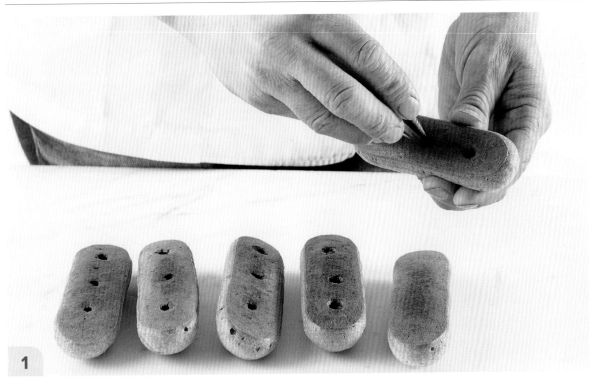

1 Using a ¼-inch (0.5 cm) round piping tip, pierce 3 evenly spaced holes in bottom of each éclair.

2 **3** **4** Place piping tip in pastry bag, if desired. Using a spatula, fill bag with filling of choice.

5

Twist the top end of the pastry bag closed and keep twisting until filling is forced into tip at the bottom of the bag.

6

If using a disposable bag, using scissors, snip off tip of pastry bag to make a hole about $\frac{1}{4}$ inch (0.5 cm) across.

7

8

Insert tip of pastry bag into the first hole and squeeze filling into hollow. Repeat with remaining holes. (You'll know you are filling éclairs properly when, as you are filling subsequent holes, a little filling comes out of the hole you just filled.)

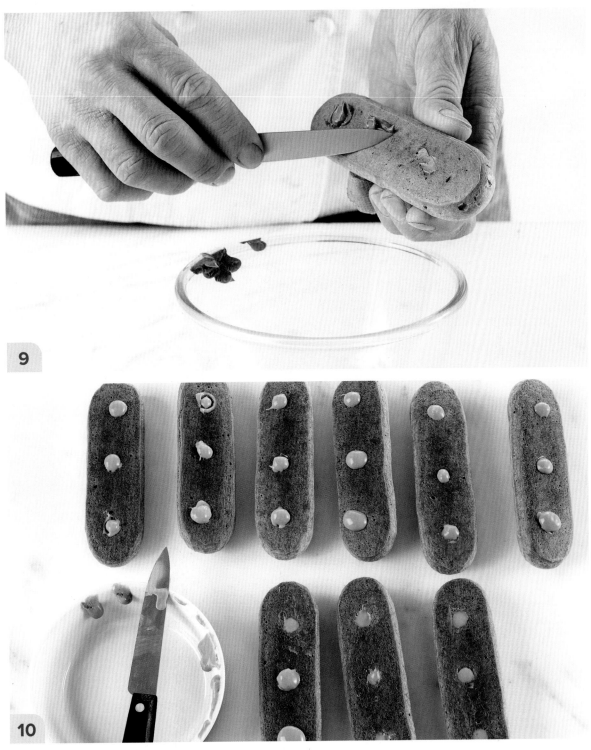

Using a small knife, scrape off excess cream.

ÉCLAIRS

Apricot Éclairs

**MAKES
10 CLASSIC ÉCLAIRS**

PREPARATION TIME
Day 1: 40 minutes
Day 2: 2½ hours

EQUIPMENT
- Immersion blender
- Instant-read thermometer
- Fine-mesh sieve
- Plastic squeeze bottle or toothbrush

Prepare apricot cream and glaze the day before assembling éclairs

APRICOT CREAM

1½ tsp	unflavored gelatin powder	7 mL
5 tsp	cold water	25 mL
⅔ cup	soft dried apricots (130 g)	150 mL
6 tbsp	heavy or whipping (35%) cream	90 mL
⅔ cup	whole milk	150 mL
⅔ cup	apricot purée	150 mL
3 tbsp	granulated sugar	45 mL
5	large egg yolks	5

APRICOT GLAZE

2 tsp	unflavored gelatin powder	10 mL
2½ tbsp	cold water	37 mL
⅔ cup	heavy or whipping (35%) cream	150 mL
¼ cup	glucose syrup (60 g)	60 mL
6 oz	white chocolate, pistoles or chopped	180 g
6 oz	white compound chocolate, chopped	180 g
	Orange food coloring	

CHOUX PASTRY

½	batch Choux Pastry (page 29)	½

DECORATION

	Ruby-red edible shimmer dust or luster dust
	Red food coloring (optional)

1 APRICOT CREAM

In a small bowl, stir together gelatin and cold water. Set aside.

1

Chop apricots into small pieces.

2

In a saucepan, combine cream and milk and bring to a boil over medium heat. Add apricots and stir to combine. Remove from heat and set aside for 15 minutes, until apricots are softened and plump.

3

Using immersion blender, purée until smooth.

4

Add apricot purée.

5

6

In a small bowl, whisk together sugar and egg yolks. Add to apricot mixture. Cook over low heat, stirring constantly, until mixture thickens slightly and reaches 180°F (82°C). It should be the consistency of crème anglaise (custard sauce).

7

8

Remove from heat, add gelatin mixture and stir until dissolved.

Pour mixture through fine-mesh sieve into a shallow dish.

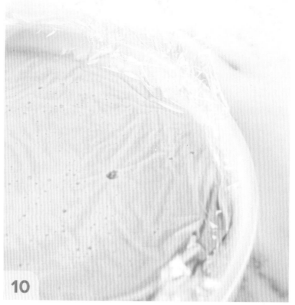

Press to extract liquid; discard solids. Cover surface with plastic wrap (to prevent skin from forming) and refrigerate until well chilled, for up to 1 day.

2 APRICOT GLAZE

In a small bowl, stir together gelatin and cold water. Set aside.

In a saucepan, combine cream and glucose syrup and bring to a boil over medium heat. Remove from heat and stir in gelatin mixture.

In a bowl set over a saucepan of water simmering over low heat, melt white and compound chocolate, stirring occasionally, until smooth. Remove from heat.

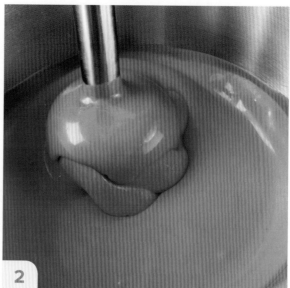

Add cream mixture to melted chocolate. Using immersion blender, blend until smooth. While mixing, add just enough food coloring to tint to an apricot color. Cover surface with plastic wrap and refrigerate until well chilled, for up to 1 day.

CHOUX PASTRY

Prepare choux pastry and bake éclairs following Steps 1 to 9 on pages 30 and 31, and Steps 1 to 4 on page 33.

 ## DECORATION

Pour a small amount of ruby-red shimmer dust into a ramekin.

 ## ASSEMBLY

Using a ¼-inch (0.5 cm) round piping tip, pierce 3 evenly spaced holes in bottom of each éclair.

Place piping tip in pastry bag, if desired. Using a spatula, fill pastry bag with apricot cream. Fill éclairs, inserting a small quantity of cream in each hole. Using a small knife, remove excess cream. (See technique on pages 47 to 49.)

In a bowl set over a saucepan of water simmering over low heat, heat glaze, stirring occasionally, until it reaches 90°F (32°C) and has a smooth, shiny texture.

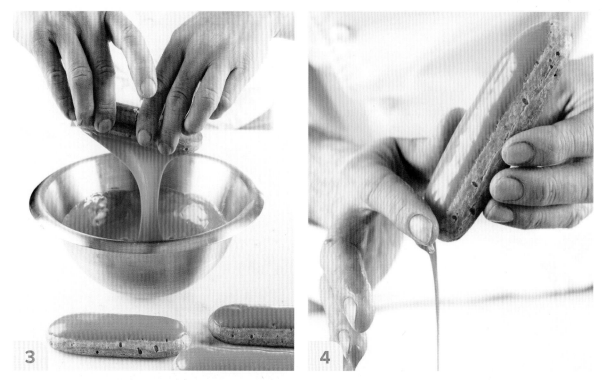

Dip the top of each éclair in glaze and remove excess with a finger.

Using the tip of a paring knife, pick up a small amount of shimmer dust. Hold the knife near the end of each éclair and, using an empty plastic squeeze bottle, blow dust onto top of each éclair. If a speckled effect is desired, in a small bowl, dissolve a little red food coloring in a small amount of water. Dip a toothbrush into coloring and, holding it bristle side up, rub bristles with the edge of a palette knife, splattering color over éclair until you obtain the desired effect. Let stand until glaze is set.

Caramel Éclairs

**MAKES
10 CLASSIC ÉCLAIRS**

PREPARATION TIME
Day 1: 1 hour
Day 2: 2 hours

EQUIPMENT
- Immersion blender
- Instant-read and/or candy thermometer

*Prepare
caramel cream
the day before
assembling
éclairs*

CARAMEL CREAM

¾ tsp	unflavored gelatin powder	3 mL
2½ tsp	cold water	12 mL
⅔ cup	heavy or whipping (35%) cream	150 mL
½ tsp	fleur de sel	2 mL
9 tbsp	granulated sugar (120 g), divided	135 mL
⅓ cup	unsalted butter	75 mL
8 oz	mascarpone cheese	235 g

CHOUX PASTRY

½	batch Choux Pastry (page 29)	½

CARAMEL FONDANT

7 tbsp	heavy or whipping (35%) cream	105 mL
2½ tbsp	glucose syrup (35 g)	35 mL
¼ cup	granulated sugar (50 g)	60 mL
2 tsp	salted butter	10 mL
8 oz	prepared fondant	250 g

DECORATION

3½ oz	milk chocolate–coated popping candy or crispy milk chocolate pearls	100 g
	Bronze shimmer dust or luster dust	

1 CARAMEL CREAM

In a small bowl, stir together gelatin and cold water. Set aside.

1

2

In a small bowl, combine cream and fleur de sel.

In a saucepan, melt half of the sugar over medium heat, without stirring. Boil without stirring until it turns brown, then add remaining sugar and stir to dissolve. Boil until it turns a deep caramel color.

3

4

5

Add cream mixture and stir to combine.

Add butter and stir until completely melted. Turn off heat.

Add gelatin mixture and stir until dissolved.

6

Using immersion blender, blend until smooth.

7

Transfer mixture to a small bowl and let cool to 113°F (45°C).

8

9

In a bowl, combine mascarpone and half of the cooled caramel. Using a spatula, beat until blended and smooth.

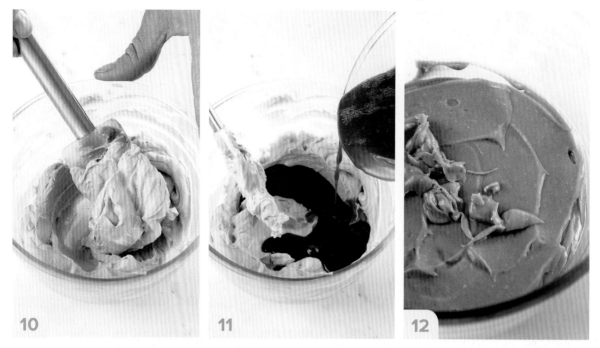

10

11

12

Beat in remaining caramel until well blended and no lumps remain. Cover surface of caramel cream with plastic wrap and refrigerate until chilled, for up to 1 day.

2 CHOUX PASTRY

Prepare choux pastry and bake éclairs following Steps 1 to 9 on pages 30 and 31, and Steps 1 to 4 on page 33.

3 CARAMEL FONDANT

In a small saucepan, warm cream over medium heat.

1

2

In a medium saucepan, warm glucose syrup over medium heat.

Gradually add sugar to glucose syrup, while stirring, and heat until melted.

3

Boil, stirring occasionally, just until mixture turns a light caramel color.

4

Pour in warm cream (cream needs to be warm so caramel doesn't seize), stirring to combine.

5

Boil caramel, without stirring, until it reaches 228°F (109°C).

6

Remove saucepan from heat. Add butter and fondant.

7

Using a wooden spoon, stir until mixture is smooth and shiny. Set aside and let cool to 99°F (37°C).

4 DECORATION

In a small bowl, combine popping candy and a few pinches of bronze shimmer dust.

5 ASSEMBLY

Using a ¼-inch (0.5 cm) round piping tip, pierce 3 evenly spaced holes in base of each éclair.

Place piping tip in pastry bag, if desired. Using a spatula, fill pastry bag with prepared caramel cream. Fill each éclair, inserting a small quantity of cream in each hole. Using a small knife, remove excess cream. (See technique on pages 47 to 49.)

Once fondant has cooled to 99°F (37°C), dip the top of each éclair in fondant and remove excess with a finger.

Working quickly, arrange pieces of popping candy on top of éclairs, before fondant forms a crust. Let stand until fondant is set.

Black Currant Éclairs

**MAKES
10 CLASSIC ÉCLAIRS**

PREPARATION TIME
Day 1: 40 minutes
Day 2: 2 hours

EQUIPMENT
- Immersion blender
- Instant-read thermometer
- Mini pastry bag

Prepare black currant cream and violet glaze the day before assembling éclairs

BLACK CURRANT CREAM

1½ tsp	unflavored gelatin powder	7 mL
5 tsp	cold water	25 mL
⅔ cup	black currant purée (205 g)	150 mL
⅓ cup	granulated sugar (64 g)	75 mL
7½ oz	mascarpone cheese	210 g

VIOLET GLAZE

2 tsp	unflavored gelatin powder	10 mL
2½ tbsp	cold water	37 mL
⅔ cup	heavy or whipping (35%) cream	150 mL
¼ cup	glucose syrup (60 g)	60 mL
6 oz	white chocolate, pistoles or chopped	180 g
6 oz	white compound chocolate	180 g
	Violet food coloring	

CHOUX PASTRY

½	batch Choux Pastry (page 29)	½

DECORATION

1	bar (1½ to 2 oz/45 to 60 g) hazelnut milk chocolate	1
1 cup + 3 tbsp	confectioners' (icing) sugar (150 g)	295 mL
	Violet food coloring, preferably powdered	
	Black currant jelly	

1 BLACK CURRANT CREAM

In a small bowl, stir together gelatin and cold water. Set aside.

1

2

In a saucepan, combine black currant purée and sugar and warm over medium heat, stirring to dissolve sugar.

When the mixture reaches 140°F (60°C), remove pan from heat. Add gelatin mixture and stir until gelatin is dissolved. Transfer to a bowl and let cool to 117°F (47°C).

3

4

Add mascarpone to cooled black currant mixture and stir with a spatula until well incorporated. Cover surface with plastic wrap and refrigerate until chilled, for up to 1 day.

2 VIOLET GLAZE

In a small bowl, stir together gelatin and cold water. Set aside.

In a saucepan, combine cream and glucose syrup and bring to a boil over medium heat. Remove from heat and stir in gelatin mixture until gelatin is dissolved.

In a heatproof bowl set over a saucepan of water simmering over low heat, melt white chocolate and compound, stirring occasionally, until smooth. Remove from heat.

Add cream mixture to melted chocolate. Using immersion blender, blend, gradually adding just enough food coloring to make a dark violet color, until smooth. Cover surface with plastic wrap and refrigerate until chilled, for up to 1 day.

3 CHOUX PASTRY

Prepare choux pastry and bake éclairs following Steps 1 to 9 on pages 30 and 31, and Steps 1 to 4 on page 33.

4 DECORATION

Using a sharp knife, cut chocolate bar into small cubes. Set aside.

In a bowl, whisk together confectioners' sugar and just enough violet food coloring to color sugar purple.

Roll chocolate cubes between the palms of your hands to form balls. Roll each ball in violet sugar until well coated.

5 ASSEMBLY

Using a ¼-inch (0.5 cm) round piping tip, pierce 3 evenly spaced holes in base of each éclair.

Place piping tip in pastry bag, if desired. Using a rubber spatula, fill pastry bag with prepared black currant cream. Fill each éclair, inserting a small quantity of cream in each hole. Using a small knife, remove excess cream. (See technique on pages 47 to 49.)

In a bowl set over a saucepan of water simmering over low heat, reheat violet glaze, stirring occasionally, until it reaches 90°F (32°C). Dip the top of each éclair in glaze and remove excess with a finger.

Decorate the top of each éclair with 3 violet chocolate balls.

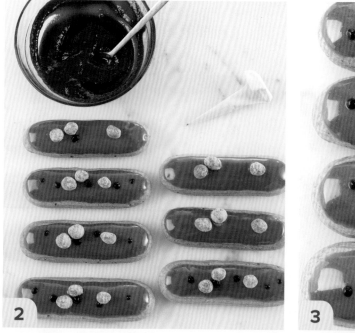
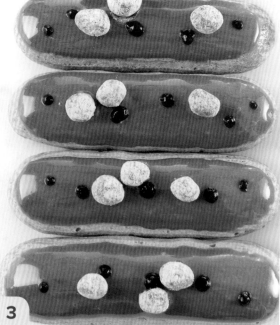

Fill a mini pastry bag with black currant jelly and place a few drops around each ball. Let stand until glaze is set.

Chocolate Coconut Éclairs

<table>
<tr><td style="background:#888;color:white">MAKES
10 CLASSIC ÉCLAIRS</td></tr>
</table>

PREPARATION TIME
Day 1: 40 minutes
Day 2: 2 hours

EQUIPMENT
- Immersion blender
- Instant-read thermometer

> **Prepare white chocolate glaze the day before assembling éclairs**

WHITE CHOCOLATE GLAZE

2 tsp	unflavored gelatin powder	10 mL
2½ tbsp	cold water	37 mL
⅔ cup	heavy or whipping (35%) cream	150 mL
¼ cup	glucose syrup (60 g)	60 mL
6 oz	white chocolate, pistoles or chopped	180 g
6 oz	white compound chocolate, chopped	180 g
2 tsp	food-grade titanium dioxide powder or rice starch (optional)	10 mL

CHOUX PASTRY

½	batch Choux Pastry (page 29)	½

COCONUT CREAM

1¾ tsp	unflavored gelatin powder	8 mL
2 tbsp	cold water	30 mL
1⅓ cups	coconut milk	325 mL
6 tbsp	heavy or whipping (35%) cream	90 mL
2 oz	white couverture chocolate, pistoles or chopped	60 g

ASSEMBLY
Chocolate glaze

14 oz	milk chocolate, chopped	400 g
7 oz	milk chocolate, pistoles or chopped	200 g

Decoration

1 tsp	silver shimmer dust or luster dust	5 mL
1⅓ cups	sweetened desiccated coconut (125 g)	325 mL

1 WHITE CHOCOLATE GLAZE

In a small bowl, combine gelatin and cold water. Set aside.

In a saucepan, combine cream and glucose syrup and bring to a boil over medium heat. Remove from heat and stir in gelatin mixture until gelatin is dissolved.

Place white chocolate in a heatproof bowl. In a saucepan, melt compound chocolate over medium heat. Pour over chocolate in bowl. Add warm cream mixture and whisk well until chocolate is melted.

Using immersion blender, blend glaze while adding titanium oxide (if using), until smooth. Cover surface with plastic wrap and refrigerate until chilled, for up to 1 day.

2 CHOUX PASTRY

Prepare choux pastry and bake éclairs following Steps 1 to 9 on pages 30 and 31, and Steps 1 to 4 on page 33.

3 COCONUT CREAM

In a small bowl, combine gelatin and cold water. Set aside.

In a saucepan, whisk together coconut milk and cream and bring to a boil over medium heat. Remove from heat and add gelatin mixture, stirring until dissolved.

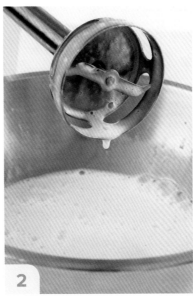

1	2	3
Place white chocolate in a heatproof bowl and pour in warm coconut milk mixture; whisk until chocolate is melted.	Using immersion blender, blend until smooth.	Transfer mixture to a shallow dish. Cover surface with plastic wrap and refrigerate until chilled, for up to 1 day.

4 ASSEMBLY

Using a ¼-inch (0.5 cm) round piping tip, pierce 3 evenly spaced holes in base of each éclair.

Place piping tip in pastry bag, if desired. Using a spatula, fill pastry bag with prepared coconut cream. Fill each éclair, inserting a small quantity of cream in each hole. Using a small knife, remove excess cream. (See technique on pages 47 to 49.) Transfer to a baking sheet and refrigerate until needed.

In a bowl set over a saucepan of water simmering over low heat, melt 14 oz (400 g) milk chocolate until it reaches 104°F (40°C), stirring until smooth. Remove from heat. Add 7 oz (200 g) milk chocolate pistoles and stir until melted and smooth.

Dip the top of each éclair in melted chocolate and remove excess with a finger. Transfer to a baking sheet and refrigerate until set.

3

In bowl set over a saucepan of water simmering over low heat, reheat white chocolate glaze, stirring occasionally, until melted but not too runny. Remove from heat.

4

Using immersion blender, blend until smooth and shiny.

5

Working quickly, gently dip just the tops of each chocolate-coated éclair in white glaze, being careful not to totally cover the chocolate glaze. Transfer to baking sheet and let stand for a few minutes, until glaze is slightly set.

6

Meanwhile, in a bowl, stir together shimmer dust and coconut.

7

Dip the top of each éclair into coconut mixture, pressing down gently so coconut adheres well to white glaze. Let stand until glaze is set.

Chocolate Éclairs

PREPARATION TIME

Day 1: 1 hour

Day 2: 2 hours

EQUIPMENT

- Instant-read thermometer
- 2 flexible steel sheets or very smooth, flat baking sheets (each 20 by 12 inches/50 by 30 cm)
- 1 sheet (20 by 12 inches/50 by 30 cm) acetate (for chocolate work)
- Long offset palette knife
- Large pastry brush with soft bristles

Prepare cocoa glaze the day before assembling éclairs

COCOA GLAZE

1½ tsp	unflavored gelatin powder	7 mL
5 tsp	cold water	25 mL
6 tbsp	water	90 mL
½ cup	granulated sugar (100 g)	125 mL
¼ cup	heavy or whipping (35%) cream	60 mL
⅔ cup	unsweetened cocoa powder (40 g)	150 mL

CHOUX PASTRY

½	batch Choux Pastry (page 29)	½

CHOCOLATE CREAM

2	large egg yolks	2
3 tbsp	granulated sugar	45 mL
1½ tbsp	cornstarch	22 mL
¾ cup + 1 tbsp	whole milk	190 mL
3 tbsp	heavy or whipping (35%) cream	45 mL
2¾ oz	dark (70%) chocolate	80 g
1½ tbsp	unsalted butter, cut into pieces	22 mL

CHOCOLATE PIECES

15½ oz	dark (70%) chocolate, pistoles or chopped, divided	450 g
	Gold shimmer dust or luster dust	

1 COCOA GLAZE

In a small bowl, stir together gelatin and cold water. Set aside.

1

In a saucepan, combine water and sugar and bring to a boil over medium heat, stirring until sugar is dissolved. While whisking, gradually pour in cream. Return to a boil.

2

Add cocoa powder, while whisking. Boil for 2 minutes, whisking constantly to prevent sticking.

3

Remove from heat and set aside to cool slightly (until about 140°F/60°C). Add gelatin mixture and stir until gelatin is dissolved. Using an immersion blender, blend until smooth.

4

Transfer glaze to a bowl, cover surface with plastic wrap and refrigerate until chilled, for up to 1 day.

2 CHOUX PASTRY

Prepare choux pastry and bake éclairs following Steps 1 to 9 on pages 30 and 31, and Steps 1 to 4 on page 33.

ᕃ CHOCOLATE CREAM

1

In a bowl, whisk together egg yolks and sugar until frothy. Whisk in cornstarch. Set aside.

2

In a saucepan, combine milk and cream and bring to a boil over medium heat. Remove from heat.

3

While whisking, gradually pour a little of the warm milk mixture into egg mixture to warm the eggs. Then gradually whisk egg mixture into remaining milk mixture in pan.

4

Return pan to medium heat and cook, whisking constantly, until mixture thickens enough to adhere to whisk.

5

Place chocolate in a bowl. Add thickened cream mixture and whisk until chocolate is completely melted and mixture is smooth. Set aside to cool to 104°F (40°C).

6

Add butter in pieces and, using immersion blender, blend until mixture is smooth and shiny. Cover surface with plastic wrap and refrigerate until chilled, for up to 1 day.

4 CHOCOLATE PIECES

1

2

3

In a bowl set over a saucepan of water simmering over low heat, melt 10 1/2 oz (300 g) of the chocolate pistoles, stirring occasionally. Remove from heat. Add remaining 5 oz (150 g) chocolate pistoles and stir until melted and smooth.

Test the texture by dipping the tip of a knife into it. The chocolate should be slightly thick and perfectly smooth. (If too thin, let cool; if too thick, gently place over hot water to warm slightly.)

Cover one of the steel sheets with acetate. Pour melted chocolate in center of sheet.

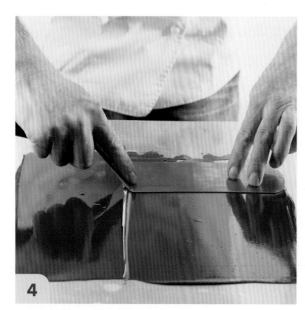

4

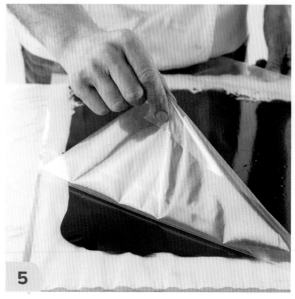

5

Working quickly, use offset palette knife to spread a thin layer of chocolate over entire sheet. Your movement should be quick and firm. Cover chocolate with a sheet of parchment paper, then place second steel sheet on top. Place a weight on top and transfer to freezer for about 10 minutes to harden.

Once hardened, flip over metal sheets so acetate is on top of the chocolate. Carefully peel off acetate. During chilling, a thin film of water will have formed on the surface of the chocolate; this will help the gold shimmer dust to stick to it.

6 **7**

Pour shimmer dust into a ramekin. Using large pastry brush, lightly dust about $\frac{3}{5}$ of one side of the chocolate sheet with the shimmer dust until you achieve a sparkly, translucent finish. Using the tines of a fork, lightly scrape the other half of the chocolate to create a textured surface.

5 ASSEMBLY

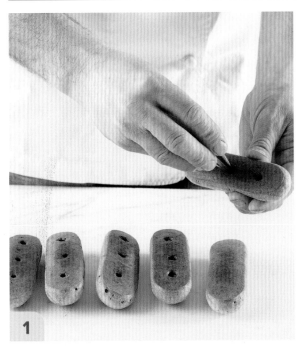

1 **2**

Using a $\frac{1}{4}$-inch (0.5 cm) round piping tip, pierce 3 evenly spaced holes in base of each éclair.

Place piping tip in pastry bag, if desired. Using a rubber spatula, fill pastry bag with prepared chocolate cream. Fill each éclair, inserting a small quantity of cream in each hole.

3

Using a small knife, remove excess cream. (See techniques on pages 47 to 49.) In a heatproof bowl set over a saucepan of water simmering over low heat, reheat cocoa glaze, stirring occasionally, until completely smooth. Dip the top of each éclair in glaze and remove excess with a finger. Set aside.

4

Using a sharp knife, cut out 30 gold and 20 textured chocolate squares, each about $\frac{2}{3}$ inch (1.5 cm) in size.

5

Using the tip of a knife, start by placing one gold square at one end of a chocolate éclair. Continue in an alternating pattern of gold and textured squares, so that each éclair is topped with three gold and two chocolate squares. Let stand until glaze is set.

Chocolate Crunch Éclairs

<table>
<tr><td>

**MAKES
10 CLASSIC ÉCLAIRS**

PREPARATION TIME
Day 1: 1 hour
Day 2: 1½ hours

EQUIPMENT
- Immersion blender
- Instant-read thermometer
- Fine-mesh sieve

Prepare
milk chocolate
cream and glaze
the day before
assembling
éclairs

</td></tr>
</table>

MILK CHOCOLATE CREAM

4¼ oz	milk chocolate, pistoles or chopped	120 g
1 cup + 1 tbsp	whole milk	265 mL
¼ cup	heavy or whipping (35%) cream	60 mL
3	large egg yolks	3
3 tbsp	granulated sugar (40 g)	45 mL
3 tbsp	cornstarch (24 g)	45 mL
¼ cup	unsalted butter, cut into cubes (55 g)	60 mL

MILK CHOCOLATE GLAZE

1½ tsp	unflavored gelatin powder	7 mL
5 tsp	cold water	25 mL
3 tbsp + 1 tsp	glucose syrup (50 g)	50 mL
½ cup	heavy or whipping (35%) cream	125 mL
5 oz	milk chocolate, pistoles or chopped	150 g
5 oz	white compound chocolate	150 g

CHOUX PASTRY

½	batch Choux Pastry (page 29)	½

DECORATION

6 oz	chocolate-coated popping candy or crispy dark chocolate pearls	175 g
	Silver shimmer dust or luster dust	

MILK CHOCOLATE CREAM

Place chocolate in a heatproof bowl.

In a saucepan, combine milk and cream and bring to a boil over medium heat. Remove from heat and set aside.

In another bowl, whisk together egg yolks and sugar until creamy and thick. Add cornstarch and whisk to combine. While whisking, pour a little of the warm milk mixture into egg mixture (this will warm the egg mixture and prevent it from cooking).

While whisking, add warmed egg mixture to the pan with remaining milk mixture.

Cook, whisking constantly, just until mixture comes to a boil and thickens.

Pour hot milk mixture over chocolate and, using a rubber spatula, stir until chocolate is melted and mixture is smooth. Insert thermometer into chocolate mixture and set aside to cool slightly.

Once cream cools to 104°F (40°C), add butter, a few cubes at a time, using immersion blender to blend after each addition, until mixture is smooth and creamy.

Transfer chocolate cream to a shallow dish, cover surface with plastic wrap and refrigerate until chilled, for up to 1 day.

2 MILK CHOCOLATE GLAZE

In a small bowl, stir together gelatin and cold water. Set aside.

1

In a saucepan, combine glucose syrup and cream and heat over medium heat until warm.

2

Add gelatin and stir until gelatin is dissolved. Set aside.

3

In a heatproof bowl set over a pan of water simmering over low heat, melt milk chocolate and white compound, stirring until smooth. Remove from heat and gradually pour in cream mixture, whisking until smooth.

4

Using immersion blender, blend until smooth and shiny. Cover surface with plastic wrap and refrigerate until chilled, for up to 1 day.

3 CHOUX PASTRY

Prepare choux pastry and bake éclairs following Steps 1 to 9 on pages 30 and 31, and Steps 1 to 4 on page 33.

4 DECORATION

Pour popping candy through fine-mesh sieve to collect the largest pieces; save small pieces for another use. (If using pearls, omit this step.)

Transfer one-third of the candy to a small bowl. Add silver shimmer dust and stir until candy is thoroughly coated. Place remaining candy in another bowl.

5 ASSEMBLY

Using a ¼-inch (0.5 cm) round piping tip, pierce 3 evenly spaced holes in base of each éclair. Place piping tip in pastry bag, if desired. Using a rubber spatula, fill pastry bag with prepared chocolate cream. Fill each éclair, inserting a small quantity of cream in each hole. Using a small knife, remove excess cream. (See technique on pages 47 to 49.)

In bowl set over a saucepan of water simmering over low heat, reheat chocolate glaze, stirring occasionally, until it reaches 90°F (32°C). Using immersion blender, blend until smooth. Dip the top of each éclair in glaze and remove excess with a finger. Set aside.

3

Using your fingers, gently press silver popping candy down the middle of each éclair. Transfer éclairs to a baking sheet and refrigerate for 10 minutes to harden glaze.

4

Dip each éclair, glaze-side down, into remaining popping candy to cover the rest of the glaze. Let stand until glaze is set.

Hazelnut Praline Éclairs

PREPARATION TIME

Day 1: 1 hour 30 minutes

Day 2: 1 hour

EQUIPMENT

- Food processor
- Immersion blender
- Candy thermometer
- Silicone baking mat
- Serrated knife

- Preheat oven to 325°F (160°C)

Prepare hazelnut praline and praline cream the day before assembling éclairs

HAZELNUT PRALINE

1⅓ cups	blanched hazelnuts (180 g)	325 mL
9 tbsp	granulated sugar (120 g)	135 mL
3 tbsp	water	45 mL
¼ tsp	fleur de sel	1 mL

PRALINE CREAM

1 cup	whole milk	250 mL
3 tbsp	heavy or whipping (35%) cream	45 mL
3	large egg yolks	3
2½ tbsp	granulated sugar	37 mL
2 tbsp + 2 tsp	cornstarch	40 mL
6 oz	hazelnut praline	170 g
¼ cup	unsalted butter, cut into cubes (60 g)	60 mL

CHOUX PASTRY

½	batch Choux Pastry (page 29)	½
1	batch Craquelin (page 36)	1

ASSEMBLY

50	blanched hazelnuts (approx.)	50

1 HAZELNUT PRALINE

On a baking sheet in a single layer, spread 1⅓ cups (325 mL) hazelnuts and the 50 hazelnuts to be used in the assembly, keeping separate on the sheet. Toast hazelnuts in preheated oven for about 20 minutes (toasted hazelnuts should be brown in the center). Let cool slightly.

In a saucepan, combine sugar and water and bring to a boil over medium heat, stirring until sugar is dissolved. Cook, without stirring, until mixture turns a caramel color. Add 1⅓ cups (325 mL) warm toasted hazelnuts. Stir until hazelnuts are well coated, then sprinkle with fleur de sel and stir to combine.

Spread candied hazelnuts (praline) over silicone baking mat. Set aside until completely cool.

Break praline into pieces and transfer to food processor fitted with a metal blade.

Pulse until praline is ground to a powder. Process on highest speed until praline forms a smooth liquid. Transfer to a heatproof bowl and set aside.

2 PRALINE CREAM

In a saucepan, combine milk and cream and bring to a boil over medium heat. Remove from heat and set aside.

In a bowl, combine egg yolks and sugar and whisk until frothy.

Add cornstarch and whisk until combined. While whisking, pour a little of the warm milk mixture into egg mixture to warm the eggs. While whisking, add egg mixture to remaining milk mixture in pan. Bring to a boil, whisking constantly, over medium heat.

Pour mixture over prepared praline and whisk to combine.

Let cool to 104°F (40°C). Using immersion blender, gradually incorporate butter, a few pieces at a time, blending after each addition, until smooth and shiny.

Transfer praline cream to a shallow dish. Cover surface with plastic wrap and refrigerate until chilled, for up to 1 day.

3 CHOUX PASTRY

Prepare choux pastry following steps 1 to 9 on pages 30 and 31 and bake Craquelin Éclairs (page 37).

4 ASSEMBLY

Using a serrated knife, cut éclairs in half lengthwise. Place piping tip in pastry bag, if desired. Using a spatula, fill pastry bag with prepared praline cream.

Fill bottom half of each éclair.

Place 4 roasted hazelnuts on top of each éclair.

Using a spatula, lightly stir praline cream, refill pastry bag and pipe a ball of cream on top of each hazelnut. Sandwich each éclair with its top half.

Caramel Peanut Éclairs

MAKES 10 CLASSIC ÉCLAIRS

PREPARATION TIME

Day 1: 1 hour
Day 2: 2½ hours

EQUIPMENT

- Instant-read thermometer
- Immersion blender
- Large, round pastry brush

Prepare caramel cream the day before assembling éclairs

CARAMEL CREAM

¾ tsp	unflavored gelatin powder	3 mL
2½ tsp	cold water	12 mL
⅔ cup	heavy or whipping (35%) cream	150 mL
½ tsp	fleur de sel	2 mL
9 tbsp	granulated sugar (120 g), divided	135 mL
⅓ cup	unsalted butter (75 g)	75 mL
8 oz	mascarpone cheese	235 g

CHOUX PASTRY

½	batch Choux Pastry (page 29)	½

CARAMEL GLAZE

6 tbsp	heavy or whipping (35%) cream	90 mL
½ tsp	fleur de sel	2 mL
2 tbsp	glucose syrup (30 g)	30 mL
¾ cup + 2 tbsp	granulated sugar (180 g), divided	205 mL
⅔ cup	unsalted butter (150 g)	150 mL

CANDIED PEANUTS

1⅓ cups	unsalted roasted peanuts (200 g)	325 mL
¾ cup	confectioners' (icing) sugar (100 g)	175 mL
Pinch	fleur de sel	Pinch

CHOCOLATE GLAZE

1 lb 5 oz	milk chocolate, pistoles or chopped, divided	600 g

DECORATION

Bronze shimmer dust or luster dust

CARAMEL CREAM

In a small bowl, stir together gelatin and cold water. Set aside.

1

In a small bowl, combine cream and fleur de sel.

2

In a saucepan, melt half of the sugar over medium heat, without stirring. Boil without stirring until it turns brown, then add remaining sugar and stir to dissolve. Boil until it turns a deep caramel color.

3

Add cream mixture and stir to combine.

4

Add butter and stir until butter has completely melted. Turn off heat.

5

Add gelatin mixture and stir until gelatin is dissolved.

6

Using immersion blender, blend until smooth.

7

Transfer mixture to a small bowl and let cool to 113°F (45°C).

8

9

In a bowl, combine mascarpone and half of the cooled caramel. Using a spatula, beat until blended and smooth.

Beat in remaining caramel until well blended and no lumps remain. Cover surface of caramel cream with plastic wrap and refrigerate until chilled, for up to 1 day.

2 CHOUX PASTRY

Prepare choux pastry and bake éclairs following Steps 1 to 9 on pages 30 and 31, and Steps 1 to 4 on page 33.

3 CARAMEL GLAZE

In a saucepan over medium heat, warm cream, then add fleur de sel. Stir and set aside.

In a saucepan, combine glucose syrup and half the sugar. Bring to a boil over medium heat, stirring to dissolve sugar. Boil, without stirring, until it turns brown. Stir in remaining sugar. Return to a boil and let boil just for a few seconds.

Add warm cream mixture and stir to combine.

Add butter and stir until melted. Turn off heat.

Using immersion blender, blend until smooth.

Transfer mixture to a heatproof bowl. Cover surface with plastic wrap and set aside at room temperature until ready to use.

4 CANDIED PEANUTS

In a saucepan, combine peanuts and confectioners' sugar.

Cook over low heat, stirring constantly with a wooden spoon, until sugar has melted and browned and peanuts are completely coated. Remove from heat, add fleur de sel and stir to combine.

Working quickly, spread candied peanuts evenly over a marble or heatproof plastic cutting board.

Using a sharp knife, chop peanuts into small pieces and set aside to cool.

5 ASSEMBLY

Using a ¼-inch (0.5 cm) round piping tip, pierce 3 evenly spaced holes in base of each éclair.

Place piping tip in pastry bag, if desired. Using a spatula, fill pastry bag with prepared caramel cream. Fill each éclair, inserting a small quantity of cream in each hole. Using a small knife, remove excess cream. (See technique on pages 47 to 49.)

Dip a rubber spatula into caramel glaze to test if it is soft enough to work with. If it seems too thick, heat it slightly.

Dip the top of each éclair in caramel glaze and remove excess with a finger. Set aside.

4

Using your fingers, press chopped peanuts onto top of each éclair. Transfer finished éclairs to a baking sheet and refrigerate for 20 minutes to set.

6 CHOCOLATE GLAZE

1

2

3

In a heatproof bowl set over a saucepan of water simmering over low heat, melt 14 oz (400 g) milk chocolate, stirring occasionally. Remove from heat and add remaining 7 oz (200 g) chocolate.

Stir until completely melted. Using immersion blender, blend until smooth.

Dip the top of each prepared éclair in melted chocolate to cover peanuts and caramel glaze. Transfer to a baking sheet and refrigerate until chocolate hardens.

7 DECORATION

Pour a little bronze shimmer dust into a bowl. Using pastry brush, dust each éclair with shimmer dust until surface is very shiny.

Lemon Éclairs

PREPARATION TIME

Day 1: 20 minutes
Day 2: 2½ hours

EQUIPMENT

- Immersion blender
- Fine-toothed grater or citrus zester
- Electric mixer
- Instant-read thermometer
- 2 metal spacers (¼ inch/ 4 mm), optional
- Rolling pin
- Silicone baking mat
- Piping tip (¼ inch/0.5 cm)

Prepare yellow glaze the day before assembling éclairs

YELLOW GLAZE

2 tsp	unflavored gelatin powder	10 mL
2½ tbsp	cold water	37 mL
⅔ cup	heavy or whipping (35%) cream	150 mL
¼ cup	glucose syrup (60 g)	60 mL
6 oz	white chocolate, pistoles or chopped	180 g
6 oz	white compound chocolate, chopped	180 g
	Yellow food coloring	

CHOUX PASTRY

½	batch Choux Pastry (page 29)	½

LEMON CREAM

¾ tsp	unflavored gelatin powder	3 mL
2½ tsp	cold water	12 mL
2	large eggs	2
9 tbsp	granulated sugar (115 g)	135 mL
1 to 2	lemons	1 to 2
¾ cup	unsalted butter, cut into cubes (175 g)	175 mL

HAZELNUT STREUSEL

¼ cup	unsalted butter, softened (65 g)	60 mL
¼ tsp	fleur de sel	1 mL
½ cup	confectioners' (icing) sugar (65 g)	125 mL
⅔ cup	lightly toasted ground hazelnuts (65 g)	150 mL
½ cup	all-purpose flour (65 g)	125 mL

SWISS MERINGUE

2	large egg whites	2
1 cup + 2 tbsp	confectioners' (icing) sugar, sifted, divided (140 g)	280 mL

1 YELLOW GLAZE

In a small bowl, stir together gelatin and cold water. Set aside.

1

In a saucepan, combine cream and glucose syrup and bring to a boil over medium heat.

2

Remove from heat and stir in prepared gelatin, stirring until gelatin is dissolved.

3

In a heatproof bowl set over a saucepan of water simmering over low heat, melt white chocolate and compound, stirring occasionally, until melted and smooth. Remove from heat and stir in cream mixture.

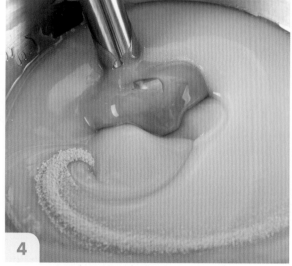

4

Using immersion blender, blend, incorporating food coloring, until bright yellow and smooth. Cover surface with plastic wrap and refrigerate until chilled, for up to 1 day.

2 CHOUX PASTRY

Prepare choux pastry and bake éclairs following Steps 1 to 9 on pages 30 and 31, and Steps 1 to 4 on page 33.

3 LEMON CREAM

In a small bowl, stir together gelatin and cold water. Set aside.

1

2

3

In a heatproof bowl, whisk together eggs and sugar.

Finely grate zest from 1 lemon, then squeeze enough juice from lemons to make ½ cup (125 mL). Add zest and juice to egg mixture.

4

5

Set bowl over a saucepan of water simmering over low heat. Cook, whisking constantly, until mixture reaches 180°F (82°C). Remove from heat and stir in prepared gelatin mixture, stirring until gelatin is dissolved. Let cool to 104°F (40°C).

Add cubed butter and, using immersion blender, blend until butter is incorporated and mixture is smooth. Transfer to a shallow dish, cover surface with plastic wrap and refrigerate until chilled.

In a bowl, using a wooden spoon, cream together butter, fleur de sel and confectioners' sugar. Stir in hazelnuts and then flour. Continue stirring until blended into a paste.

5

Cover a clean work surface with a sheet of parchment paper. If using, place two spacers parallel to each other, about 8 inches (20 cm) apart. Place hazelnut paste in center.

6

Cover paste with another sheet of parchment paper. Using rolling pin, roll out paste to just less than ¼ inch (4 mm) thick.

7

Carefully remove top sheet of parchment paper. Slide rolled paste, on parchment, onto a baking sheet and refrigerate for 30 minutes to set. Meanwhile, preheat oven to 325°F (160°C). Line a second baking sheet with parchment paper.

8

Using narrow end of piping tip like a cookie cutter, cut out balls of hazelnut paste and place them in a single layer on prepared baking sheet, spacing apart. Bake in preheated oven for about 8 minutes, until golden brown. Let hazelnut balls cool on pan on a wire rack.

5 SWISS MERINGUE

Preheat oven to 195°F (90°C). Line a baking sheet with a silicone baking mat.

1

In a heatproof bowl set over a saucepan of water simmering over low heat, whisk together egg whites and 1 cup (120 g/250 mL) confectioners' sugar. Heat, whisking constantly, until mixture reaches 113°F (45°C). Remove from heat.

2

Using electric mixer at high speed, beat until meringue is slightly firm.

3

Add remaining 2 tbsp (20 g/30 mL) confectioners' sugar and stir mixture, lifting it several times with a spatula, until soft peaks form that slump over slightly.

4

Place ¼-inch (0.5 cm) piping tip in pastry bag. Using a spatula, fill bag with meringue. Pipe small (about ¼ inch/0.5 cm) balls of meringue onto prepared baking sheet. Bake in preheated oven for 10 minutes, then turn off oven and let meringues dry in oven for 1 hour.

6 | ASSEMBLY

Using a ¼-inch (0.5 cm) round piping tip, pierce 3 evenly spaced holes in base of each éclair. Place piping tip in pastry bag, if desired. Using a spatula, fill pastry bag with prepared lemon cream. Fill each éclair, inserting a small quantity of lemon cream in each hole. Using a small knife, remove excess cream. (See technique on pages 47 to 49.)

In a bowl set over a saucepan of water simmering over low heat, reheat yellow glaze, stirring occasionally, until it reaches 90°F (32°C). Using immersion blender, blend until smooth.

Dip the top of each éclair in glaze.

Remove excess glaze with a finger.

5

Transfer éclairs to a baking sheet and refrigerate for 20 minutes to set.

6

Decorate each éclair with 3 meringue dots and 3 hazelnut streusel balls (the glaze will act as glue to help them stick). Let stand until glaze is set.

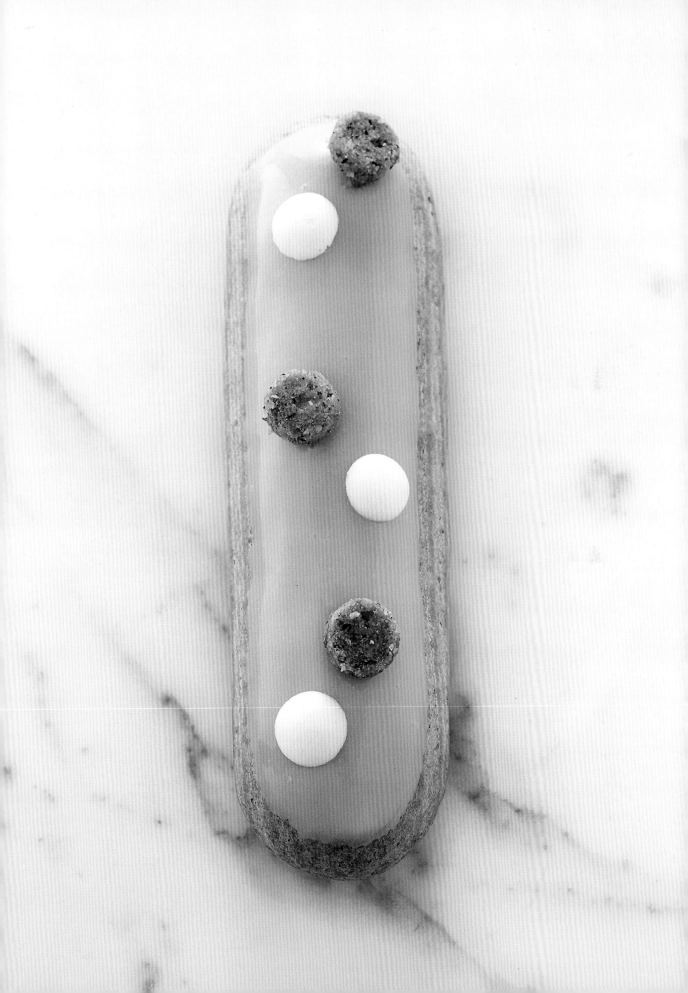

Raspberry-Cherry Sugared Almond Éclairs

PREPARATION TIME

Day 1: 1 hour
Day 2: 2½ hours

EQUIPMENT

- Immersion blender
- Instant-read or candy thermometer
- Rolling pin

Prepare almond cream and pink glaze the day before assembling éclairs

ALMOND CREAM

1½ tsp	unflavored gelatin powder	7 mL
5 tsp	cold water	25 mL
9 tbsp	whole milk	135 mL
7 tbsp	heavy or whipping (35%) cream	105 mL
1½ oz	white couverture chocolate, pistoles or chopped	45 g
1¼ oz	almond paste, cut into cubes	40 g

PINK GLAZE

1½ tsp	unflavored gelatin powder	7 mL
5 tsp	cold water	25 mL
7 tbsp	heavy or whipping (35%) cream	105 mL
2 tbsp + 2 tsp	glucose syrup (40 g)	40 mL
8 oz	white couverture chocolate, pistoles or chopped	240 g
	Red food coloring	

CHOUX PASTRY

½	batch Choux Pastry (page 29)	½

RASPBERRY-CHERRY CONFIT

⅓ cup	granulated sugar (60 g), divided	75 mL
¾ tsp	low-methoxyl pectin, such as Pomona's Universal Pectin (2 g)	3 mL
3½ tbsp	raspberry purée (70 g)	52 mL
2 tbsp	sour cherry purée, preferably Morello (40 g)	30 mL
2 tbsp	glucose syrup (30 g)	30 mL

DECORATION

1½ oz	white sugared almonds	45 g
20	raspberries	20

1 ALMOND CREAM

In a small bowl, stir together gelatin and cold water. Set aside.

In a saucepan, combine milk and cream and bring to a boil over medium heat. Stir in gelatin mixture, stirring until gelatin is dissolved. Remove from heat.

In a bowl, combine white chocolate and almond paste. Add hot cream mixture and whisk until chocolate has melted. Using immersion blender, blend until smooth.

Transfer mixture to a shallow dish. Cover surface with plastic wrap and refrigerate until chilled, for up to 1 day.

2 PINK GLAZE

In a small bowl, stir together gelatin and cold water. Set aside.

In a saucepan, combine cream and glucose syrup and bring to a boil over medium heat. Remove from heat and stir in gelatin mixture, stirring until gelatin is dissolved.

In a heatproof bowl set over a saucepan of water simmering over low heat, melt white chocolate, stirring occasionally, until melted and smooth. Remove from heat and whisk in cream mixture.

Add just enough red food coloring to turn mixture pink.

Using immersion blender, blend until smooth, adding more food coloring if necessary to obtain desired color. Cover surface with plastic wrap and refrigerate until chilled, for up to 1 day.

3 CHOUX PASTRY

Prepare choux pastry and bake éclairs following Steps 1 to 9 on pages 30 and 31, and Steps 1 to 4 on page 33.

1

In a bowl, combine one-third of the sugar and pectin.

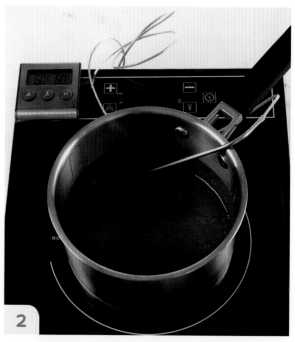

2

In a saucepan, combine raspberry and cherry purées, remaining sugar and glucose syrup. Cook, stirring, over medium heat until mixture reaches 140°F (60°C).

3

4

5

Stir in pectin mixture and bring to a boil, stirring. Boil for a few seconds. Remove from heat. Using immersion blender, blend until smooth.

Transfer mixture to a bowl. Cover with plastic wrap and refrigerate until ready to use.

5 ASSEMBLY

Using a ¼-inch (0.5 cm) round piping tip, pierce 3 evenly spaced holes in base of each éclair. Place piping tip in pastry bag, if desired. Using a spatula, fill pastry bag with prepared almond cream. Fill another pastry bag with raspberry-cherry confit.

Fill each éclair three-quarters full, inserting a small quantity of cream in each hole. Finish filling with raspberry-cherry confit (reserve remainder for decoration). Using a small knife, remove excess confit. (See techniques on pages 47 to 49.)

In bowl set over a saucepan of water simmering over low heat, reheat pink glaze, stirring occasionally, until it reaches 90°F (32°C). Remove from heat. Using immersion blender, blend until smooth.

Dip the top of each éclair in glaze and remove excess with a finger. Transfer éclairs to a baking sheet and refrigerate for 20 minutes, until almost set.

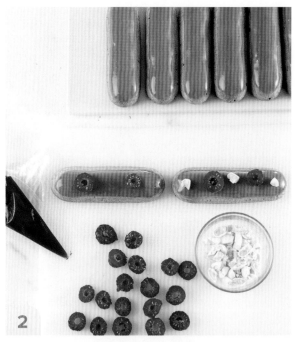

1

Place sugared almonds in a pastry bag or resealable plastic bag and, using a rolling pin, crush them into pieces.

2

Decorate each éclair with 2 raspberries (stem side up) and 3 pieces of sugared almond.

3

Fill each raspberry with a drop of reserved raspberry-cherry confit. Let stand until glaze is set.

Valentine Heart Éclairs

PREPARATION TIME

Day 1: 1 hour
Day 2: 2½ hours

EQUIPMENT

- Instant-read thermometer
- Immersion blender
- Silicone baking mat
- Cardstock, about 1 inch (2.5 cm) larger than an éclair
- White paper, about 1 inch (2.5 cm) larger than two éclairs side by side
- Tracing paper, about 1 inch (2.5 cm) larger than two éclairs side by side
- Utility knife
- 2 small spacers (1/16 inch/ 2 mm), optional
- Rolling pin
- Offset palette knife
- Airbrush (optional)
- Fine-mesh sieve
- Flat pastry brush

Prepare chocolate praline cream the day before assembling éclairs

CHOCOLATE PRALINE CREAM

Cream

¾ cup + 1 tbsp	whole milk	190 mL
3 tbsp	heavy or whipping (35%) cream	45 mL
2	large egg yolks	2
2½ tbsp	granulated sugar (30 g)	37 mL
1½ tbsp	cornstarch	22 mL
2½ oz	dark (70%) chocolate	75 g
2½ tbsp	unsalted butter, cut into cubes	37 mL

Hazelnut praline

1⅓ cups	blanched hazelnuts (180 g)	325 mL
9 tbsp	granulated sugar (120 g)	135 mL
3 tbsp	water	45 mL
¼ tsp	fleur de sel	1 mL

CHOUX PASTRY

½	batch Choux Pastry (page 29)	½

ALMOND PASTE HEARTS

5¼ oz	almond paste	150 g
	Confectioners' (icing) sugar	
	Red liquid food coloring, gel or paste	
	Neutral-flavored spirit, such as vodka (optional)	
	Gold shimmer dust	
½ cup	clear glaze (100 g)	125 mL

1 CHOCOLATE PRALINE CREAM

In a saucepan, combine milk and cream and bring to a boil over medium heat.

Meanwhile, in a bowl, whisk together egg yolks, sugar and cornstarch. While whisking, pour a little of warm milk mixture into egg mixture (this will warm the egg mixture and prevent it from cooking). Then add warmed egg mixture to the pan with remaining milk mixture. Cook, whisking constantly, until thickened.

Place chocolate in a heatproof bowl. Pour in hot milk mixture and stir until chocolate is melted and smooth. Let cool to 104°F (40°C).

Using immersion blender, gradually incorporate butter, blending after each addition, until smooth and shiny.

Prepare hazelnut praline (see page 98).

1

2

Once chocolate cream has cooled, stir in prepared hazelnut praline. Cover surface with plastic wrap and refrigerate until chilled, for up to 1 day.

2 CHOUX PASTRY

Prepare choux pastry and bake éclairs following Steps 1 to 9 on pages 30 and 31, and Steps 1 to 4 on page 33.

3 ALMOND PASTE HEARTS

1

Make templates: Trace an oblong shape the same size as your éclairs onto cardstock then cut out. Cut a sheet of white paper about 1 inch (2.5 cm) larger than two éclairs lined up side by side; cut a sheet of tracing paper the same size. Lay cardstock template on white paper and trace the outline. Move template next to the shape you have just drawn, then trace the outline again (you should end up with two side-by-side oblongs). Using utility knife, cut out the double oblong. This oblong will act as one of your stencils.

2

Place tracing paper on top of your double oblong stencil and carefully draw a heart so that each side of the heart is on one half of each oblong (see photo).

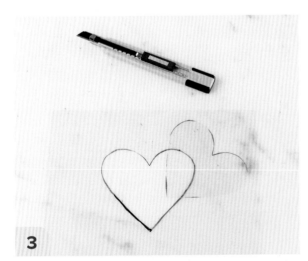

3

Using utility knife, cut out heart from middle of tracing paper (discard cut-out heart). The tracing paper will serve as another stencil.

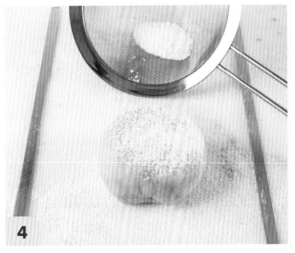

4

Sprinkle a clean work surface with confectioners' sugar. If using, place two spacers parallel to each other, about 8 inches (20 cm) apart, on work surface. Place almond paste between spacers and sprinkle with a little more confectioners' sugar to keep it from sticking.

5

Using rolling pin, roll out almond paste to ¹⁄₁₆ inch (2 mm) thick.

6

Remove spacers and carefully slide offset palette knife underneath sheet of almond paste to loosen it from work surface. Place double-oblong template on top of sheet and carefully cut out 5 double oblongs.

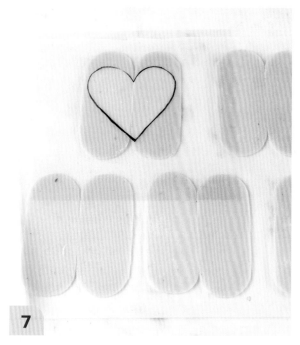

7

Center heart stencil on top of one almond paste double oblong.

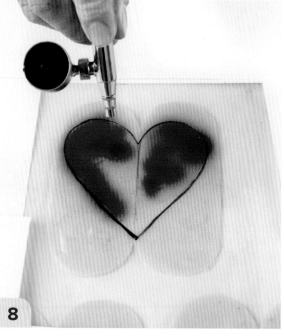

8

Fill airbrush with red food coloring. Spray coloring on almond paste to fill in heart shape. Alternatively, in a small bowl, combine a small amount of neutral spirit and red food coloring to make an intense red dye. Using pastry brush, dab onto almond paste or use a small paintbrush to paint inside heart shape.

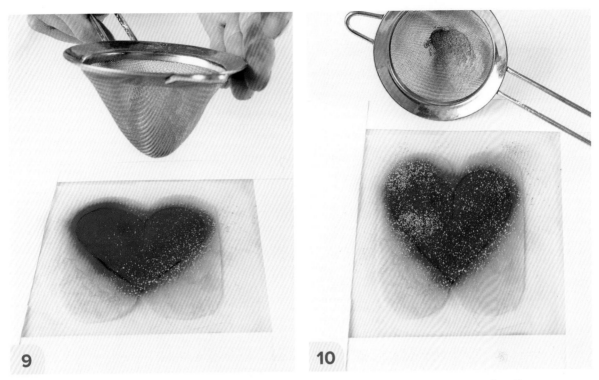

Pour a little shimmer dust into fine-mesh sieve and tap it over the heart to cover it with a fine golden film.

Gently remove heart stencil. Repeat process for remaining almond paste double oblongs. Let dry for 20 to 25 minutes before continuing with assembly.

4 ASSEMBLY

Using a ¼-inch (0.5 cm) round piping tip, pierce 3 evenly spaced holes in base of each éclair. Place piping tip in pastry bag, if desired. Using a spatula, fill pastry bag with prepared chocolate praline cream. Fill each éclair, inserting a small quantity of cream in each hole. Using a small knife, remove excess cream. (See techniques on pages 47 to 49.)

1

In a heatproof bowl set over a saucepan of water simmering over low heat, warm clear glaze. Using pastry brush, coat underside of each piece of almond paste with glaze.

2

Using a sharp knife, separate double oblongs. Place one oblong on each éclair, glazed side down.

3

4

Dip the top of each éclair in clear glaze and remove excess with your finger. Transfer éclairs to a baking sheet and refrigerate for 20 minutes to set. To serve, place two éclairs side by side to form a heart.

Fig Éclairs

PREPARATION TIME
Day 1: 1 hour
Day 2: 1½ hours

EQUIPMENT
- Immersion blender
- Instant-read thermometer
- Fine-mesh sieve

Prepare
fig cream
and violet glaze
the day before
assembling
éclairs

FIG CREAM

1½ tsp	unflavored gelatin powder	7 mL
5 tsp	cold water	25 mL
4 oz	soft dried figs	120 g
¾ cup	whole milk	175 mL
6 tbsp	heavy or whipping (35%) cream	90 mL
⅔ cup	fresh fig purée (175 g)	150 mL
2½ tbsp	granulated sugar (32 g)	37 mL
3	large egg yolks	3
	Red food coloring	

VIOLET GLAZE

2 tsp	unflavored gelatin powder	10 mL
2½ tbsp	cold water	37 mL
⅔ cup	heavy or whipping (35%) cream	150 mL
¼ cup	glucose syrup (60 g)	60 mL
6 oz	white chocolate, pistoles or chopped	180 g
6 oz	white compound chocolate, chopped	180 g
	Violet food coloring	
	Red food coloring	

CHOUX PASTRY

½	batch Choux Pastry (page 29)	½

DECORATION

	Fig seeds (reserved from cream recipe)
	Gold shimmer dust or luster dust

1 FIG CREAM

In a small bowl, stir together gelatin and cold water. Set aside.

1

Using a sharp knife, cut figs into small pieces. Set aside.

2

In a saucepan, combine milk and cream and bring to a boil over medium heat. Stir in chopped figs. Remove from heat and set aside for 20 minutes to soak.

3

Using immersion blender, blend until smooth.

4

Add fig purée and stir to combine.

In a bowl, whisk together sugar and egg yolks. Gradually add to fig mixture while stirring. Return to medium heat and cook, stirring constantly, until mixture thickens slightly and reaches 180°F (82°C). Remove from heat.

Add gelatin mixture and stir until gelatin is dissolved. Add just enough red food coloring to turn mixture slightly pink. Blend again.

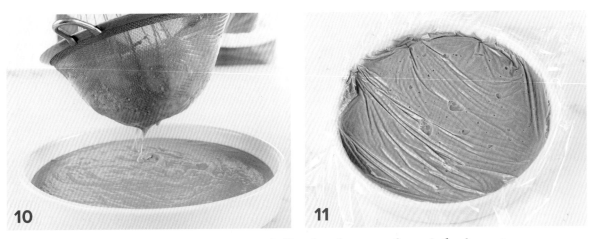

Strain mixture through fine-mesh sieve into a shallow bowl; reserve fig seeds for decoration. Cover surface of fig cream with plastic wrap and refrigerate until chilled, for up to 1 day. Cover and refrigerate fig seeds separately.

2 VIOLET GLAZE

In a small bowl, stir together gelatin and cold water. Set aside.

1

In a saucepan, combine cream and glucose syrup and bring to a boil over medium heat. Remove from heat and stir in gelatin mixture, stirring until gelatin is dissolved.

2

In a heatproof bowl, combine white chocolate and compound. Add warm cream mixture and, using a spatula, stir until chocolate is melted and smooth.

3

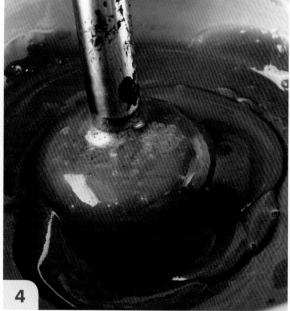

4

Using immersion blender, blend mixture until smooth. While mixing, add just enough red and violet food coloring to turn mixture reddish purple. Cover surface with plastic wrap and refrigerate until chilled, for up to 1 day.

3 CHOUX PASTRY

Prepare choux pastry and bake éclairs following Steps 1 to 9 on pages 30 and 31, and Steps 1 to 4 on page 33.

4 DECORATION

Preheat oven to 250°F (120°C). Line a baking sheet with parchment paper.

Place reserved fig seeds in a bowl and cover with hot water.

Strain rinsed fig seeds through fine-mesh sieve (discard liquid). Spread seeds over prepared baking sheet. Dry in preheated oven for 45 minutes. Transfer seeds to a bowl and let cool completely.

Once cooled, pass dried seeds through fine-mesh sieve to remove husks. Collect only the seeds and transfer to a small bowl.

Add gold shimmer dust to seeds and stir until evenly coated. Set aside.

5 ASSEMBLY

Using a ¼-inch (0.5 cm) round piping tip, pierce 3 evenly spaced holes in base of each éclair.

Place piping tip in pastry bag, if desired. Using a spatula, fill pastry bag with prepared fig cream. Fill each éclair, inserting a small quantity of cream in each hole. Using a small knife, remove excess cream. (See techniques on pages 47 to 49.)

In a bowl set over a saucepan of water simmering over low heat, reheat glaze, stirring occasionally, until it reaches 90°F (32°C). Remove from heat. Using immersion blender, blend until smooth and shiny.

Dip the top of each éclair in glaze and remove the excess with a finger.

Lightly sprinkle each éclair with golden fig seeds. Transfer éclairs to a baking sheet and refrigerate for 20 minutes to set.

Strawberry Éclairs

MAKES 10 CLASSIC ÉCLAIRS

PREPARATION TIME
Day 1: 1 hour
Day 2: 2 hours

EQUIPMENT
- Electric mixer
- Instant-read thermometer
- Small food processor

- Preheat oven to 325°F (160°C)

> Prepare pistachio paste and ganache the day before assembling éclairs

PISTACHIO PASTE (MAKES 3½ OZ/100 G)

¾ cup	shelled unsalted raw pistachios (100 g)	175 mL
4 tsp	grapeseed oil	20 mL

PISTACHIO GANACHE

¾ tsp	unflavored gelatin powder	3 mL
2½ tsp	cold water	12 mL
1 cup + 3 tbsp	heavy or whipping (35%) cream	295 mL
2½ oz	white chocolate, pistoles or chopped	65 g
1½ oz	pistachio paste	40 g

CHOUX PASTRY

½	batch Choux Pastry (page 29)	½

STRAWBERRY COULIS

6 tbsp	strawberry purée (130 g)	90 mL
1½ tbsp	lime purée or lime curd (25 g)	22 mL
7 tbsp	granulated sugar (90 g), divided	105 mL
¾ tsp	pectin powder	3 mL
1½ tsp	orange flower water	7 mL

CANDIED PISTACHIOS

¼ cup	shelled unsalted raw pistachios (30 g)	60 mL
1½ tbsp	granulated sugar (15 g)	22 mL

ASSEMBLY

10	whole strawberries	10
¾ cup	whole strawberries (125 g)	175 mL
	Fresh mint leaves	

1 PISTACHIO PASTE

Spread pistachios on a baking sheet and toast in preheated oven for 15 minutes, until browned. Transfer to a bowl and let cool. Using food processor fitted with the metal blade, process until fine. Add grapeseed oil and pulse until smooth. Use immediately or transfer to an airtight container and refrigerate until ready to use.

2 PISTACHIO GANACHE

In a small bowl, stir together gelatin and cold water. Set aside.
In a saucepan, bring cream to a boil over medium heat.

1

2

3

Remove from heat and add gelatin mixture, whisking until gelatin is dissolved.

In a heatproof bowl, combine white chocolate and 1½ oz (40 g) prepared pistachio paste (reserve remainder for another use). Pour in hot cream mixture.

4

5

6

Whisk until chocolate is melted.

Using an immersion blender, blend until smooth.

Transfer to a shallow dish, cover surface with plastic wrap and refrigerate overnight.

3 CHOUX PASTRY

Prepare choux pastry and bake éclairs following Steps 1 to 9 on pages 30 and 31, and Steps 1 to 4 on page 33.

4 STRAWBERRY COULIS

1

2

In a saucepan, combine strawberry purée, lime purée and two-thirds of the sugar.

Heat over medium heat, stirring to dissolve sugar, until mixture reaches 140°F (60°C).

3

4

Meanwhile, in a small bowl, combine remaining sugar and pectin powder. Whisk into strawberry mixture and bring to a boil, stirring. Stir in orange flower water. Remove from heat and let cool slightly. Transfer to an airtight container and refrigerate until chilled before using, for at least 2 hours or up to 1 day.

5 CANDIED PISTACHIOS

1

In a saucepan, combine pistachios and sugar.

2

Cook over low heat, stirring constantly with a wooden spoon, until sugar has melted and turned dark amber and nuts are completely coated.

3

Working quickly, spread candied pistachios evenly over a marble or heatproof plastic cutting board and let cool completely.

4

Once cooled, using a sharp knife, roughly chop pistachios.

6 ASSEMBLY

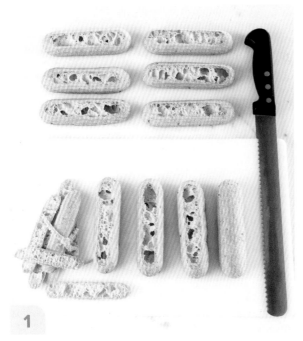

1

Using a sharp paring knife, cut off top third of each éclair (reserve tops for another use or discard). Using your fingers, scoop out soft insides and discard.

2

Slice 10 whole strawberries lengthwise and set aside. Chop ¾ cup (125 g/175 mL) strawberries into small pieces.

3

In a bowl, combine chopped strawberries and prepared strawberry coulis.

4

Using a spoon, fill each éclair with strawberry mixture. Set aside.

5

6

In bowl of electric mixer fitted with the whisk attachment, beat pistachio ganache until stiff.

Place star piping tip in pastry bag. Using a spatula, transfer whipped ganache to bag. Pipe a line of small stars to completely cover strawberry filling.

7

8

Place a slice of strawberry between each piped star.

Finish by decorating with candied pistachios and fresh mint leaves.

Raspberry Éclairs

**MAKES
10 CLASSIC ÉCLAIRS**

PREPARATION TIME
Day 1: 1 hour
Day 2: 2 hours

EQUIPMENT
- Instant-read thermometer
- Immersion blender

Prepare raspberry cream and raspberry glaze the day before assembling éclairs

RASPBERRY CREAM

1 tsp	unflavored gelatin powder	5 mL
4 tsp	cold water	20 mL
²⁄₃ cup	raspberry purée (210 g)	150 mL
1	large egg	1
4	large egg yolks	4
¹⁄₃ cup	granulated sugar (65 g)	75 mL
¹⁄₃ cup	butter, cut into cubes (80 g)	75 mL

RASPBERRY GLAZE

2 tsp	unflavored gelatin powder	10 mL
2¹⁄₂ tbsp	cold water	37 mL
²⁄₃ cup	heavy or whipping (35%) cream	150 mL
¹⁄₄ cup	glucose syrup (60 g)	60 mL
6 oz	white compound chocolate, chopped	180 g
	Red food coloring	

CHOUX PASTRY

¹⁄₂	batch Choux Pastry (page 29)	¹⁄₂

DECORATION

3¹⁄₂ oz	freeze-dried raspberries	100 g
	Red shimmer dust or luster dust	

RASPBERRY CREAM

In a small bowl, stir together gelatin and cold water. Set aside.

1

In a saucepan, heat raspberry purée over medium heat.

2

Meanwhile, in a bowl, whisk together eggs, egg yolks and sugar.

3

While whisking, gradually pour egg and sugar mixture into raspberry purée.

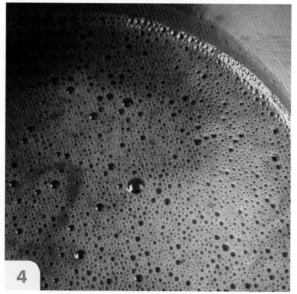

4

Heat mixture, whisking constantly, until it reaches 180°F (82°C). Stir in gelatin mixture, stirring until gelatin is dissolved. Remove from heat and transfer to a bowl.

Add butter. Using immersion blender, blend until smooth.

Transfer mixture to a shallow dish. Cover surface with plastic wrap and refrigerate until chilled, for up to 1 day.

2 RASPBERRY GLAZE

In a small bowl, stir together gelatin and cold water. Set aside.

In a saucepan, combine cream and glucose syrup and bring to a boil over medium heat. Remove from heat and stir in gelatin mixture, stirring until gelatin is dissolved.

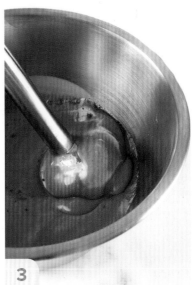

In a heatproof bowl set over a saucepan of water simmering over low heat, melt compound white chocolate. Remove from heat and add cream mixture. Using immersion blender, blend until smooth, adding just enough food coloring to turn mixture red. Cover surface with plastic wrap and refrigerate until chilled, for up to 1 day.

3 CHOUX PASTRY

Prepare choux pastry and bake éclairs following Steps 1 to 9 on pages 30 and 31, and Steps 1 to 4 on page 33.

4 DECORATION

Chop dried raspberries into small pieces and transfer to a bowl. Add a few pinches of ruby red shimmer dust and stir until raspberries are well coated.

5 ASSEMBLY

Using a ¼-inch (0.5 cm) round piping tip, pierce 3 evenly spaced holes in base of each éclair. Place piping tip in pastry bag, if desired. Using a spatula, fill pastry bag with prepared raspberry cream.

1

Fill each éclair, inserting a small quantity of raspberry cream in each hole. Using a small knife, remove excess cream. (See techniques on page 47 to 49.) In a heatproof bowl set over a saucepan of water simmering over low heat, reheat raspberry glaze, stirring occasionally, until it reaches 90°F (32°C). Remove from heat and, using immersion blender, blend until smooth and shiny.

2

3

4

Dip the top of each éclair in glaze and remove excess with a finger. Set aside.

Decorate each éclair with shimmer-dusted raspberries. Let stand until glaze is set.

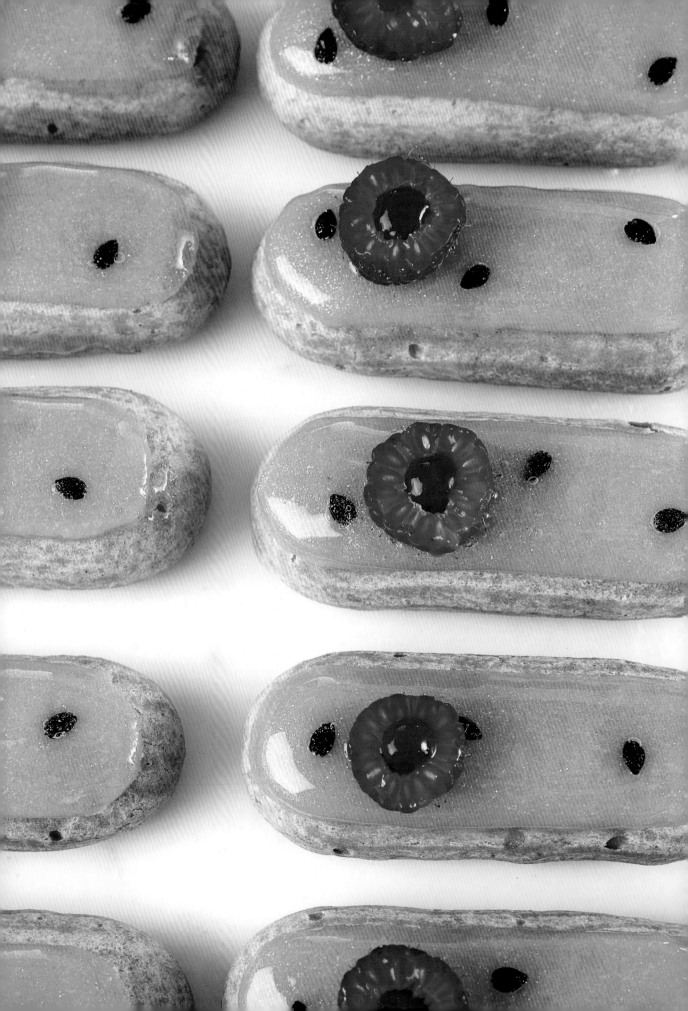

Raspberry Passion Fruit Éclairs

PREPARATION TIME

Day 1: 1 hour
Day 2: 2½ hours

EQUIPMENT

- Instant-read thermometer
- Large fine-mesh sieve
- Immersion blender
- Cardstock, about 1 inch (2.5 cm) larger than éclair
- Stand mixer or food processor
- 2 spacers (1⁄16 inch/2 mm), optional
- Rolling pin
- Offset palette knife
- Flat pastry brush
- Mini pastry bag

Prepare passion fruit cream the day before assembling éclairs

PASSION FRUIT CREAM

¾ tsp	unflavored gelatin powder	3 mL
2½ tsp	cold water	12 mL
7	purple passion fruits (approx.)	7
2	large eggs	2
2 tsp	freshly squeezed lemon juice	10 mL
6 tbsp	granulated sugar (85 g)	90 mL
⅔ cup	unsalted butter, cut into cubes (150 g)	150 mL

CHOUX PASTRY

½	batch Choux Pastry (page 29)	½

PASSION FRUIT ALMOND PASTE

7 oz	almond paste	200 g
	Orange food coloring	
	Confectioners' (icing) sugar	

ASSEMBLY

1 cup	clear glaze (200 g)	250 mL
	Gold shimmer dust or luster dust	

DECORATION

10	raspberries	10
	Raspberry jelly	

PASSION FRUIT CREAM

In a small bowl, stir together gelatin and cold water. Set aside.

1 Using a sharp knife, cut passion fruits in half. Scoop pulp into large fine-mesh sieve.

2 Using a spatula, press pulp through sieve and collect juice in a bowl; you should have about 7 tbsp (105 mL) juice. Reserve about ¼ cup (60 mL) seeds for decoration.

In a heatproof bowl, whisk eggs until blended. Add passion fruit juice and lemon juice and whisk to combine. Whisk in gelatin mixture, then sugar.

7

Set bowl over a saucepan of water simmering over low heat and cook, whisking constantly, until it reaches 180°F (82°C). Remove from heat.

8

Let cool to 104°F (40°C). Using immersion blender, blend, gradually incorporating butter cubes and mixing well after each addition.

9

Blend mixture until smooth and shiny.

10

Transfer to a shallow dish. Cover surface with plastic wrap and refrigerate until chilled, for up to 1 day.

2 CHOUX PASTRY

Prepare choux pastry and bake éclairs following Steps 1 to 9 on pages 30 and 31, and Steps 1 to 4 on page 33.

3 DRIED PASSION FRUIT SEEDS

Preheat oven to 250°F (120°C). Line a baking sheet with parchment paper.

1

Spread reserved passion fruit seeds on prepared baking sheet. Bake in preheated oven for 45 minutes, until dried. Let cool completely. Once cool, transfer to fine-mesh sieve and scrape with a rubber spatula to remove husks. Reserve seeds.

4 PASSION FRUIT ALMOND PASTE

Make a template: Trace an oblong shape the same size as your éclairs onto cardstock, then cut out.

1

2

In bowl of stand mixer fitted with paddle attachment, combine almond paste and a little orange food coloring.

Beat at low speed until well combined, adding more food coloring as needed to obtain desired color. (Or pulse in a small food processor.)

3

4

Sprinkle a clean work surface with confectioners' sugar. If using, place two spacers parallel to each other on work surface, about 8 inches (20 cm) apart. Place almond paste between spacers and sprinkle with a little more confectioners' sugar to keep it from sticking. Using rolling pin, roll out almond paste to about $^1/_{16}$ inch (2 mm) thick. Remove spacers.

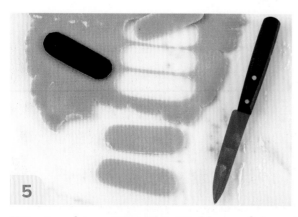

5

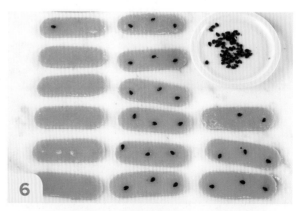

6

Using template, cut out 10 or 30 oblongs of almond paste. Carefully slide palette knife underneath oblongs to loosen. Decorate each with dried seeds, pressing down lightly to ensure they stick.

5 ASSEMBLY

Using a ¼-inch (0.5 cm) round piping tip, pierce 3 evenly spaced holes in base of each éclair.

Place piping tip in pastry bag, if desired. Using a spatula, fill pastry bag with prepared passion fruit cream. Fill each éclair, inserting a small quantity of cream in each hole. Using a small knife, remove excess cream. (See techniques on pages 47 to 49.)

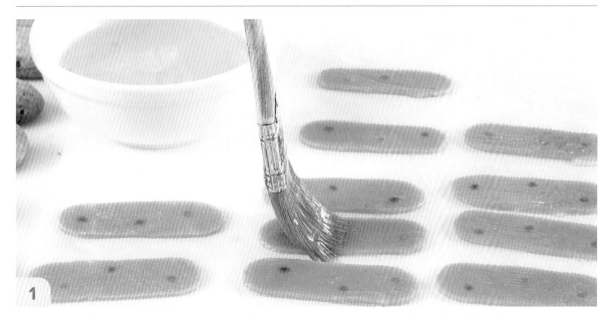

In a heatproof bowl set over a saucepan of water simmering over low heat, heat clear glaze, stirring occasionally, until completely smooth. Using a pastry brush, coat the underside (side without seeds) of each almond paste oblong with glaze (reserve remaining glaze).

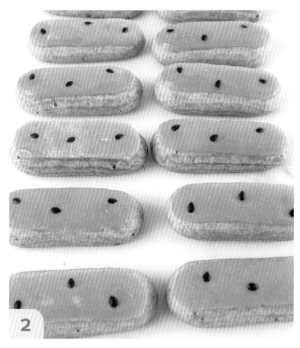

Lay an almond paste oblong on each éclair, glaze side down.

Add a little shimmer dust to remaining glaze, using the brush to stir well.

Dip the top of each éclair in glaze and gently remove excess with brush. Set aside.

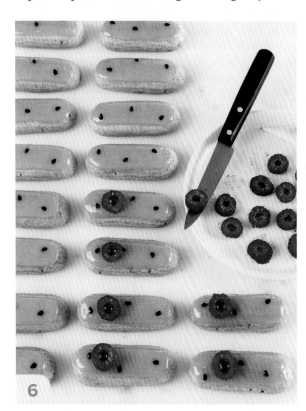

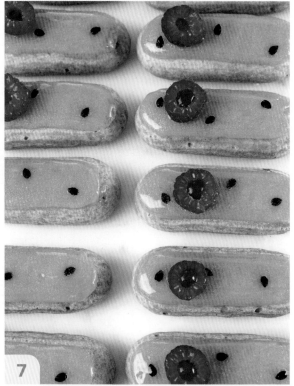

Using the tip of a knife, place 1 raspberry, stem side up, on each éclair.

Using mini pastry bag filled with raspberry jelly, fill the hole in each raspberry. Let stand until glaze is set.

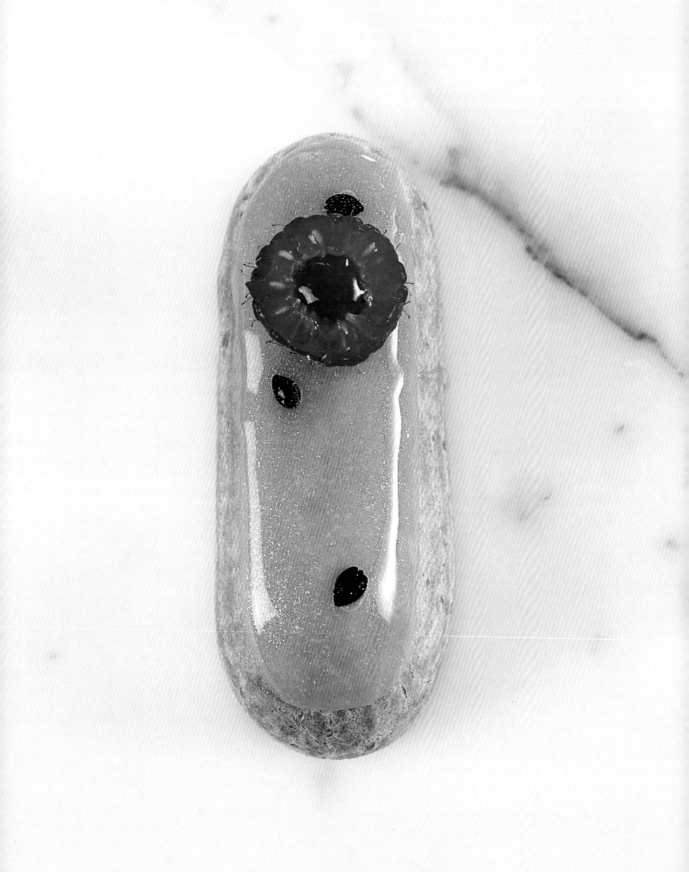

Milk Chocolate Caramel Éclairs

MAKES
10 CLASSIC ÉCLAIRS

PREPARATION TIME
Day 1: 1 hour
Day 2: 2 hours

EQUIPMENT
- Immersion blender
- Instant-read thermometer
- Fine-mesh sieve
- Large, round pastry brush

Prepare caramel chocolate cream and milk chocolate glaze the day before assembling éclairs

CARAMEL CHOCOLATE CREAM

¾ tsp	unflavored gelatin powder	3 mL
2½ tsp	cold water	12 mL
⅔ cup	granulated sugar (130 g), divided	150 mL
⅔ cup	heavy or whipping (35%) cream	150 mL
¾ tsp	fleur de sel	3 mL
⅓ cup	unsalted butter, cut into cubes (75 g)	75 mL
2 oz	dark (60%) chocolate	60 g
9½ oz	mascarpone cheese	270 g

MILK CHOCOLATE GLAZE

1½ tsp	unflavored gelatin powder	7 mL
5 tsp	cold water	25 mL
3½ tbsp	glucose syrup (50 g)	52 mL
½ cup	heavy or whipping (35%) cream	125 mL
5¼ oz	milk chocolate, pistoles or chopped	150 g
5¼ oz	white compound chocolate, chopped	150 g

CHOUX PASTRY

½	batch Choux Pastry (page 29)	½

DECORATION

	Bronze shimmer dust or luster dust	
10	milk chocolate–coated Gavottes crêpe dentelle cookies or other crispy layered cookies, such as Piroulines	10

1 CARAMEL CHOCOLATE CREAM

In a small bowl, stir together gelatin and cold water. Set aside.

In a saucepan, melt half of the sugar over medium heat, stirring just until dissolved. Boil, without stirring, until it turns brown, then add remaining sugar and stir to dissolve. Boil until it turns a deep caramel color.

Meanwhile, in another saucepan, combine cream and fleur de sel and warm over medium heat. Add to melted sugar (the mixture will bubble up) and, stirring constantly, return to a full boil.

Remove from heat. Stir in butter, gelatin mixture and chocolate, until melted. Using immersion blender, blend until smooth. Let cool to 113°F (45°C).

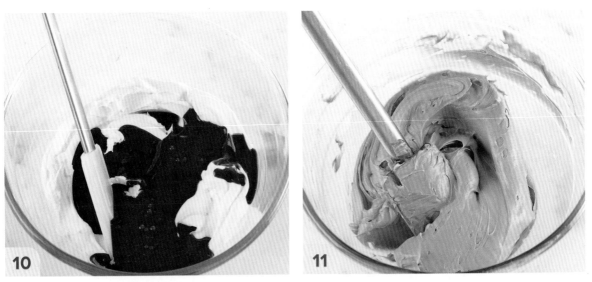

In a bowl, combine mascarpone and some of the cooled caramel; stir well.

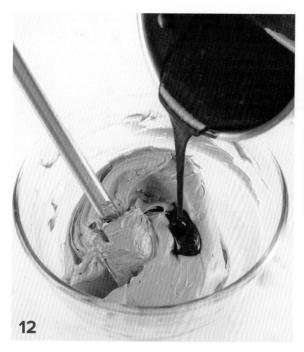

12

13

Stir in remaining caramel until blended. Cover surface with plastic wrap and refrigerate until chilled, for up to 1 day.

2 MILK CHOCOLATE GLAZE

In a small bowl, stir together gelatin and cold water. Set aside.

In a heatproof bowl set over a saucepan of water simmering over low heat, melt milk chocolate and white compound, stirring until smooth. Remove from heat and set aside.

1

2

In a saucepan, combine glucose syrup and cream and bring to a simmer over medium heat.

Stir in gelatin mixture, stirring until gelatin is dissolved.

3

While whisking, slowly add cream mixture to melted chocolate mixture.

4

Using immersion blender, blend until smooth and shiny. Cover with plastic wrap and refrigerate until chilled, for up to 1 day.

3 CHOUX PASTRY

Prepare choux pastry and bake éclairs following Steps 1 to 9 on pages 30 and 31, and Steps 1 to 4 on page 33.

4 DECORATION

1

Pour a little bronze shimmer dust into a small dish. Using large, round pastry brush, apply shimmer dust to cookies until desired effect is reached.

2

Using a sharp knife, cut each cookie into three equal pieces.

5 ASSEMBLY

Using a ¼-inch (0.5 cm) round piping tip, pierce 3 evenly spaced holes in base of each éclair.

Place piping tip in pastry bag, if desired. Using a spatula, fill pastry bag with prepared caramel chocolate cream. Fill each éclair, inserting a small quantity of cream in each hole. Using a small knife, remove excess cream. (See technique on pages 47 to 49.)

In heatproof bowl set over a saucepan of water simmering over low heat, reheat milk chocolate glaze until it reaches 90°F (32°C). Remove from heat. Using immersion blender, blend until smooth.

Dip the top of each éclair in glaze and remove excess with a finger. Transfer to a baking sheet and refrigerate for 10 minutes, until slightly set.

Arrange 3 pieces of cookie, even spaced, on top of each éclair. Let stand until glaze is set.

Chocolate Hazelnut Éclairs

PREPARATION TIME

Day 1: 1 hour

Day 2: 2 hours

EQUIPMENT

- Immersion blender
- Hand-held electric mixer
- 2 microwave-safe plastic or glass cups
- Small offset palette knife
- Stand mixer
- Fine-tooth grater
- Mini pastry bag

Prepare milk chocolate hazelnut ganache the day before assembling éclairs

MILK CHOCOLATE HAZELNUT GANACHE

¾ tsp	unflavored gelatin powder	3 mL
2½ tsp	cold water	12 mL
1 cup + 6 tbsp	heavy or whipping (35%) cream	340 mL
2 tsp	glucose syrup (10 g)	10 mL
4 oz	milk chocolate, pistoles or chopped	120 g
2 tbsp	puréed Hazelnut Praline (page 98)	30 mL

CHOUX PASTRY

½	batch Choux Pastry (page 29)	½

SOFT CARAMEL

3 tbsp	heavy or whipping (35%) cream	45 mL
Pinch	fleur de sel	Pinch
4 tsp	glucose syrup (20 g)	20 mL
6 tbsp	granulated sugar, divided (85 g)	90 mL
¼ cup	unsalted butter, cut into cubes (65 g)	60 mL
2 oz	chocolate-coated popping candy or crispy chocolate pearls	65 g

CARAMELIZED HAZELNUTS

¾ cup	blanched hazelnuts (100 g)	175 mL
6 tbsp	confectioners' (icing) sugar (50 g)	90 mL

HAZELNUT SPONGE CAKE

3 tbsp	ground hazelnuts	45 mL
2 tsp	all-purpose flour	10 mL
1½ tbsp	granulated sugar	22 mL
1	large egg, beaten	1
½ tsp	grapeseed oil	2 mL

1 MILK CHOCOLATE HAZELNUT GANACHE

In a small bowl, stir together gelatin and cold water. Set aside.

In a saucepan, combine cream and glucose syrup and bring to a boil over medium heat. Remove from heat.

Add gelatin mixture and whisk until gelatin is dissolved. Set aside.

In a heatproof bowl, combine milk chocolate and hazelnut praline. Pour in cream mixture and whisk until chocolate is melted

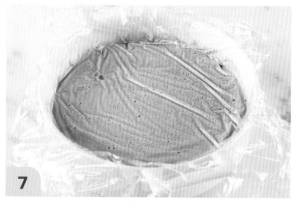

Using immersion blender, blend until smooth.

Pour mixture into a shallow dish. Cover surface with plastic wrap and refrigerate until chilled, for up to 1 day.

2 CHOUX PASTRY

Prepare choux pastry and bake éclairs following Steps 1 to 9 on pages 30 and 31, and Steps 1 to 4 on page 33.

3 SOFT CARAMEL

In a saucepan over medium heat, warm cream, then add fleur de sel. Stir and set aside.

1 / **2**
In a saucepan, combine glucose syrup and half the sugar and bring to a boil over medium heat, stirring to dissolve sugar. Boil, without stirring, until it turns brown. Stir in remaining sugar. Return to a boil and let boil just for a few seconds.

3
Add warm cream mixture and stir to combine. Add butter and stir until melted. Remove from heat.

4
Using immersion blender, blend until smooth.

5
Transfer mixture to a heatproof bowl. Cover surface with plastic wrap and set aside at room temperature until ready to use. (You will add the chocolate-coated popping candy in Step 3 of the assembly, page 182.)

4 CARAMELIZED HAZELNUTS

In a saucepan, combine hazelnuts and sugar. Cook over low heat, stirring constantly with a wooden spoon, until sugar has melted and turned dark amber and hazelnuts are completely coated.

Working quickly, spread candied hazelnuts evenly over a marble or heatproof plastic cutting board. Using offset palette knife, separate them while they are still hot. Let cool.

5 HAZELNUT SPONGE CAKE

Sift ground hazelnuts, flour and sugar into a large bowl. Using electric mixer at low speed, gradually mix in egg. Increase speed to highest setting and whip for at least 1 minute.

Reduce speed to low and drizzle in grapeseed oil. Mix until well combined.

3 Divide batter evenly between plastic or glass cups (they should be about a third full). Cook in microwave on High for 20 seconds (cake should rise to rim of cup) or until just set.

4 Remove cups from microwave, turn upside down and set aside to cool.

6 ASSEMBLY

1

2

Using a sharp serrated knife, cut off top third of each éclair (reserve tops for another use or discard). Using your fingers, scoop out insides and discard.

3

Fill a mini pastry bag with about ¼ cup (60 mL) prepared soft caramel and set aside (this will be used to decorate the éclairs). Add chocolate-coated popping candy to remaining caramel and gently stir until well combined.

4

Place a large round piping tip in pastry bag, if desired. Using a spatula, transfer remaining caramel (with popping candy) to bag. Fill each éclair half full of caramel.

5

In bowl of stand mixer fitted with the whisk attachment, whisk milk chocolate hazelnut ganache until stiff peaks form.

6

Place a ½-inch (1 cm) round tip in another pastry bag. Using a spatula, fill bag with ganache and finish filling each éclair.

7

Using small offset palette knife, smooth ganache to obtain a perfectly flat surface.

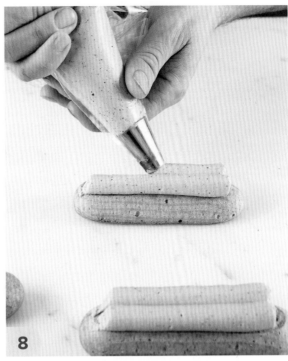

8

Pipe two parallel rows of ganache on top of each éclair.

9

Using reserved pastry bag of soft caramel, pipe a thin line between the two rows of ganache.

10

Using a sharp knife, cut candied hazelnuts in half. Set aside.

11

Unmold cooled sponge cakes from cups.

12

Tear sponge cakes into small pieces.

13

Decorate éclairs with pieces of hazelnut, reserving a few, and sponge cake.

14

To finish, using fine-tooth grater, grate a thin layer of candied hazelnut over each éclair.

Pistachio Orange Éclairs

PREPARATION TIME

Day 1: 1 hour
Day 2: 2 hours

EQUIPMENT

- Fine-mesh sieve
- Food processor
- Fine-tooth grater or citrus zester
- Instant-read thermometer
- Immersion blender
- Stand mixer
- 2 metal spacers (1/16 inch/ 2 mm), optional
- Fine-mesh sieve
- Rolling pin
- Large offset palette knife
- Cardstock, about 1 inch (2.5 cm) larger than éclair
- Wide, flat pastry brush

- Preheat oven to 325°F (160°C)

PISTACHIO PASTE

½ cup	shelled unsalted raw pistachio nuts (60 g)	125 mL
2 tsp	grapeseed oil	10 mL

PISTACHIO CREAM

¾ tsp	unflavored gelatin powder	3 mL
2½ tsp	cold water	12 mL
1 cup + 1 tbsp	whole milk	265 mL
1	orange	1
1	large egg yolk	1
3 tbsp	granulated sugar (40 g)	45 mL
2 tbsp	cornstarch	30 mL
1 tbsp	pistachio paste (recipe above)	15 mL
⅓ cup	unsalted butter, cut into cubes (80 g)	75 mL

CHOUX PASTRY

½	batch Choux Pastry (page 29)	½

PISTACHIO-ALMOND PASTE

4½ oz	almond paste, cut into cubes	130 g
2 tsp	pistachio paste (recipe above)	10 mL
	Green food coloring	
	Confectioners' (icing) sugar	

SPARKLING GREEN GLAZE

1 cup	clear glaze (200 g)	250 mL
	Green food coloring powder	
1 tbsp	gold shimmer dust or luster dust	15 mL

ASSEMBLY AND DECORATION

	Additional clear glaze
	Candied orange peel, cut into cubes (about 50)

1 PISTACHIO PASTE

Place pistachios on a baking sheet and bake in preheated oven for 10 minutes, until slightly brown in the center. Transfer to a bowl and let cool.

Once cool, transfer pistachios to food processor fitted with the metal blade and process until ground to a fine powder. Reserve about 1 tbsp (15 mL) for decoration and set aside.

Add oil to remaining ground pistachios and process until smooth. Transfer to a bowl, cover and refrigerate until ready to use.

2 PISTACHIO CREAM

In a small bowl, stir together gelatin and cold water. Set aside.

In a saucepan, bring milk to a boil over medium heat, grating zest from orange into milk as it heats. Remove from heat and cover with plastic wrap. Let steep for 10 minutes.

Meanwhile, in a heatproof bowl, combine egg yolk, sugar and cornstarch.

Whisk until mixture is creamy and thick.

5 Pour steeped milk through fine-mesh sieve into egg mixture; discard zest.

6 Return to saucepan and bring to a boil over medium heat, whisking constantly.

7 Remove from heat. Add gelatin mixture, stirring until gelatin is dissolved.

8 9 Place 1 tbsp (15 mL) pistachio paste into a heatproof bowl. Pour hot custard over pistachio paste and whisk until completely incorporated.

Let cool to 104°F (40°C). Using immersion blender, gradually incorporate butter, blending after each addition, until smooth and shiny. Transfer to a shallow dish. Cover with plastic wrap and refrigerate until chilled, for up to 1 day.

3 CHOUX PASTRY

Prepare choux pastry and bake éclairs following Steps 1 to 9 on pages 30 and 31, and Steps 1 to 4 on page 33.

4 PISTACHIO-ALMOND PASTE

In stand mixer fitted with the paddle attachment, beat cubed almond paste until smooth.

While mixing, add enough green food coloring to turn paste bright green. Add 2 tsp (10 mL) pistachio paste. Mix until smooth, adding more food coloring if necessary to achieve desired color.

4

Sprinkle a clean work surface with confectioners' sugar. If using, place two spacers parallel to each other, about 8 inches (20 cm) apart. Place prepared paste between spacers and sprinkle with a little more confectioners' sugar to keep it from sticking.

5

Using rolling pin, roll out paste to about $1/16$ inch (2 mm) thick.

6

Remove spacers, if necessary, and carefully slide offset palette knife underneath sheet of paste to loosen it from work surface.

7

Make a template: Trace an oblong shape slightly smaller than your éclairs onto cardstock, then cut out. Place the template on top of rolled-out paste and cut out 10 oblongs.

5 SPARKLING GREEN GLAZE

In a saucepan over medium heat, heat clear glaze until smooth and no lumps remain. Add just enough food coloring to turn glaze deep green. Remove from heat.

Add gold shimmer dust. Using immersion blender, blend until smooth. Set aside at room temperature.

6 ASSEMBLY

Using a ¼-inch (0.5 cm) round piping tip, pierce 3 evenly spaced holes in base of each éclair.

Place piping tip in pastry bag, if desired. Using a spatula, fill pastry bag with prepared pistachio cream. Fill each éclair, inserting a small quantity of cream in each hole. Using a small knife, remove excess cream. (See techniques on pages 47 to 49.)

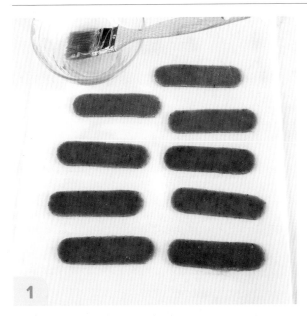

Warm a small amount of clear glaze in microwave just until fluid. Using pastry brush, coat one side of each piece of pistachio-almond paste.

Place a piece of paste, glazed side down, on each éclair, pressing down lightly on edges of paste to help it stick to the éclair.

Warm prepared sparking green glaze in microwave, if necessary to thin. Dip the top of each éclair in glaze.

Remove excess glaze by brushing lightly with pastry brush.

Decorate each éclair with a row of candied orange peel cubes bordered by a little reserved pistachio powder. Let stand until glaze is set.

Red Kiss Éclairs

PREPARATION TIME

Day 1: 1 hour
Day 2: 2 hours

EQUIPMENT

- Immersion blender
- Standard blender (optional)
- Stand mixer
- 2 metal spacers (1/16 inch/ 2 mm), optional
- Instant-read thermometer
- Rolling pin
- Large offset palette knife
- Brush
- Fine-mesh sieve
- Cardstock, about 1 inch (2.5 cm) larger than éclair

Prepare chocolate cream the day before assembling éclairs

CHOCOLATE CREAM

2	large egg yolks	2
2½ tbsp	granulated sugar (30 g)	37 mL
2 tbsp	cornstarch (15 g)	30 mL
¾ cup	whole milk	175 mL
3 tbsp	heavy or whipping (35%) cream	45 mL
2½ oz	dark (70%) chocolate, pistoles or chopped	70 g
3 tbsp	unsalted butter, cut into cubes (40 g)	45 mL

CHOUX PASTRY

½	batch Choux Pastry (page 29), colored red	½

RASPBERRY COMPOTE

1 cup	fresh raspberries (170 g)	250 mL
3 tbsp	granulated sugar (35 g), divided	45 mL
¾ tsp	pectin powder	3 mL

ALMOND PASTE

5 oz	almond paste, cut into cubes	150 g
	Red food coloring	
	Confectioners' (icing) sugar	

SPARKLING RED GLAZE

½ cup	clear glaze (100 g)	125 mL
	Red food coloring	
	Silver shimmer dust or luster dust	
	Additional clear glaze	

1

In a bowl, combine whisk together egg yolks, sugar and cornstarch until frothy. Set aside.

2

In a saucepan, combine milk and cream and bring to a boil over medium heat. While whisking, pour a little of the hot milk mixture into egg mixture (this will warm the egg mixture and prevent it from cooking). Then add warmed egg mixture to the pan with remaining milk mixture.

3

Bring to a boil, whisking. Cook, whisking constantly, until thickened. Remove from heat.

4

Place chocolate in a heatproof bowl and pour in hot milk mixture. Stir until chocolate is melted and mixture is smooth.

5

Let cool to 104°F (40°C). Using immersion blender, gradually incorporate butter, blending after each addition, until smooth and shiny. Cover with plastic wrap and refrigerate until ready to use.

2 CHOUX PASTRY

Prepare red-colored choux pastry and bake éclairs following Steps 1 to 11 and Steps 1 to 4 on pages 30 to 32, and Steps 1 to 4 on page 33.

3 RASPBERRY COMPOTE

In a tall cup, using an immersion blender, or in a standard blender at high speed, purée raspberries.

In a bowl, combine one-third of the sugar and the pectin.

1

In a saucepan, combine raspberry purée and remaining sugar. Heat over medium heat, stirring, until mixture reaches 140°F (60°C), then whisk in pectin-sugar mixture.

2

Bring to a boil, whisking constantly. Remove from heat and immediately transfer compote to a shallow dish. Cover surface with plastic wrap and refrigerate until chilled.

1

In bowl of stand mixer fitted with the paddle attachment, beat cubed almond paste until smooth. While mixing, add enough red food coloring to turn paste deep red.

2

Mix until smooth, adding more food coloring if necessary to achieve desired color.

3

Sprinkle a clean work surface with confectioners' sugar. If using, place two spacers parallel to each other, about 8 inches (20 cm) apart. Place prepared paste between spacers and sprinkle with a little more confectioners' sugar to keep it from sticking.

4

Using rolling pin, roll out paste to $\frac{1}{16}$ inch (2 mm) thick.

5

Remove spacers, if necessary, and carefully slide offset palette knife underneath sheet of paste to loosen it from work surface.

6

Make a template: Trace an oblong shape slightly smaller than your éclairs onto cardstock, then cut out. Place the template on top of rolled-out paste and cut out 10 oblongs.

5 SPARKLING RED GLAZE

1

In a saucepan, heat clear glaze over medium heat, stirring, until smooth and no lumps remain. Add just enough food coloring to turn glaze deep red. Remove from heat.

2

Add desired amount of silver shimmer dust and whisk until well combined. Remove from heat and set aside at room temperature until ready to use.

1

Using a ¼-inch (0.5 cm) round piping tip, pierce 3 evenly spaced holes across the top of each éclair.

2

Place piping tip in pastry bag, if desired. Using a spatula, fill pastry bag with prepared chocolate cream. Fill each éclair, inserting a small quantity of cream in each hole and leaving enough space to insert a little raspberry compote.

3

Whisk raspberry compote.

4

Using a spatula, fill another pastry bag with compote.

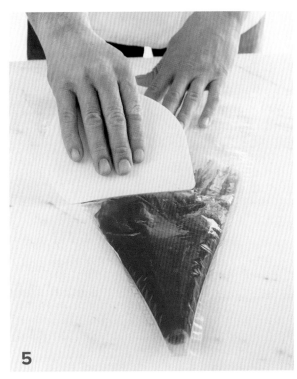

5

Using a scraper, push compote to bottom of pastry bag. Snip off tip of bag.

6

Fill éclairs with raspberry compote. Using a small knife, remove any excess filling.

7

Warm a small amount of clear glaze in microwave oven just until fluid. Using a brush, coat one side of each oblong of almond paste.

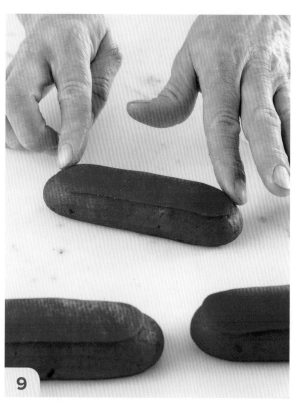

8

Place one paste oblong, glazed side down, on each éclair top, covering the holes.

9

Press down lightly on edges of the almond paste to help it stick to the éclair.

10

In a saucepan, warm prepared sparkling red glaze over low heat until soft but not runny. Dip the top of each éclair in glaze and remove excess with a finger. Let stand until glaze is set.

Vanilla Éclairs

PREPARATION TIME

Day 1: 1 hour

Day 2: 2 hours

EQUIPMENT

- Immersion blender
- Instant-read thermometer
- Fine-mesh sieve

Prepare vanilla glaze and vanilla cream the day before assembling éclairs

VANILLA GLAZE

1¾ tsp	unflavored gelatin powder	8 mL
2 tbsp	cold water	30 mL
2	vanilla beans	2
½ cup	heavy or whipping (35%) cream	125 mL
3½ tbsp	glucose syrup (50 g)	52 mL
5 oz	white chocolate, pistoles or chopped	150 g
5 oz	white compound chocolate, chopped	150 g
1½ tsp	titanium dioxide or rice starch	7 mL

VANILLA CREAM

2	vanilla beans	2
1¼ cups	whole milk	300 mL
2	large egg yolks	2
¼ cup	granulated sugar (60 g)	60 mL
2½ tbsp	cornstarch (20 g)	37 mL
7 tbsp	butter, cut into cubes (95 g)	105 mL

CHOUX PASTRY

½	batch Choux Pastry (page 29)	½

CARAMELIZED PECANS

¾ cup	chopped pecans (100 g)	175 mL
6 tbsp	confectioners' (icing) sugar	90 mL

1 VANILLA GLAZE

In a small bowl, stir together gelatin and cold water. Set aside.

In a heatproof bowl set over a saucepan of water simmering over low heat, melt white chocolate and compound, stirring until smooth. Remove from heat.

Using a sharp knife, slice vanilla beans in half lengthwise and scrape out seeds; reserve pods and seeds.

In a saucepan, combine cream and glucose syrup and bring to a boil over medium heat. Add vanilla bean pods and seeds and stir well.

Remove from heat, cover with plastic wrap and let steep for 20 minutes.

Add gelatin mixture and whisk until gelatin is dissolved. Pour mixture through fine-mesh sieve into a bowl. Rub vanilla beans with a whisk to collect as many seeds as possible. Remove pods, rinse and reserve for another use; discard any other solids.

6

Add melted chocolate mixture to strained cream mixture.

7

Using immersion blender, blend until smooth. While blending, add titanium dioxide. Cover surface with plastic wrap and refrigerate until chilled, for up to 1 day.

2 VANILLA CREAM

Using a sharp knife, slice vanilla beans in half lengthwise and scrape out seeds; reserve pods and seeds.

1

2

3

In a saucepan, bring milk to a boil over medium heat. Add reserved vanilla bean pods and seeds. Remove from heat. Cover with plastic wrap and let steep for 20 minutes. Remove pods, rinse and save for another use. Set milk aside.

In a bowl, whisk together egg yolks, sugar and cornstarch until creamy and thick.

While whisking, pour a little of the warm milk mixture into egg mixture (this gently warms the egg mixture and prevents it from cooking). Then add warmed egg mixture to pan with remaining vanilla milk.

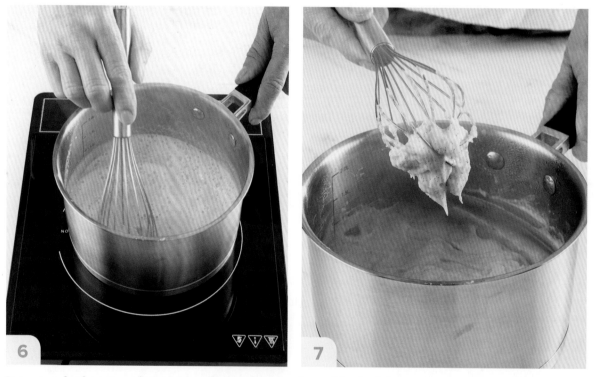

Bring to a boil over medium heat, whisking constantly, and let boil for 1 minute, until it thickens.

Let cool to 104°F (40°C). Using immersion blender, gradually incorporate butter, blending after each addition, until smooth and shiny.

Transfer mixture to a shallow dish, cover surface with plastic wrap and refrigerate for least 2 hours or preferably overnight.

3 CHOUX PASTRY

Prepare choux pastry and bake éclairs following Steps 1 to 9 on pages 30 and 31, and Steps 1 to 4 on page 33.

◢ CARAMELIZED PECANS

In a saucepan, combine pecans and confectioners' sugar. Cook over low heat, stirring constantly, until sugar has melted and turned dark amber and pecans are completely coated.

Working quickly, spread candied pecans over a marble or heatproof plastic cutting board. Let cool.

Separate the pecans, using your hands.

5 ASSEMBLY

In a heatproof bowl set over a saucepan of water simmering over low heat, reheat vanilla cream, stirring occasionally, to thin slightly, if necessary. Remove from heat.

Using a ¼-inch (0.5 cm) round piping tip, pierce 3 evenly spaced holes in base of each éclair.

Place piping tip in pastry bag, if desired. Using a spatula, fill pastry bag with vanilla cream. Fill each éclair, inserting a small quantity of cream in each hole. (See techniques on pages 47 to 49.)

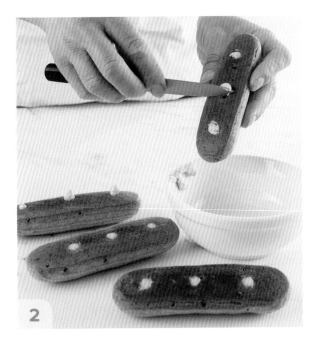

Using a small knife, remove excess cream.

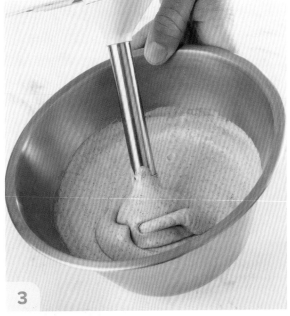

In a heatproof bowl set over a saucepan of water simmering over low heat, reheat vanilla glaze, stirring occasionally, until it reaches 90°F (32°C). Remove from heat. Using immersion blender, blend until smooth and shiny.

Dip the top of each éclair in glaze and remove excess with a finger. Transfer to a baking sheet and refrigerate for about 10 minutes to set.

Decorate the top of each éclair with pieces of candied pecans. Let stand until glaze is set.

ACKNOWLEDGMENTS

My heartfelt thanks to Jean-Pierre for his work,
devotion and good spirits.

Thanks to the team at La Martinière, especially
Laure Aline for her commitment and Florence Lecuyer
for her trust.

Many thanks to Rina for her expert eye and beautiful work.

Thanks to Marie, who worked on the editing
and proofreading.

Thanks as well to Karine for her patience and kindness.

Finally, a hug to each member of my team at L'Éclair
de génie for their self-assurance and steadfastness.

Index

N

P

R

S

V

Library and Archives Canada Cataloguing in Publication

Adam, Christophe, 1972-
[Éclairs. English]
   Éclairs : easy, elegant & modern recipes / Christophe Adam.

Includes index.
"Originally published under the title Les éclairs ©2015, Éditions de la Martinière,
   une marque de la société EDLM (Paris)."--Title page verso.
Translation of: Les éclairs.
ISBN 978-0-7788-0567-0 (softcover)

   1. Pastry. 2. Desserts. 3. Baking. 4. Cookbooks. I. Title. II. Title: Éclairs. English.

TX773.A4313 2017   641.86'59   C2016-907918-X